the student LEADERSHIP GUIDE

4th edition

brendon burchard

EXPERTS ACADEMY PRESS

An Imprint of Morgan James Publishing

Lthe**student** EADERSHIP GUIDE

4th edition

Published in New York, New York, by Morgan James Publishing. Morgan James and The Entrepreneurial Publisher are trademarks of Morgan James, LLC. www.MorganJamesPublishing.com

The Morgan James Speakers Group can bring authors to your live event. For more information or to book an event visit The Morgan James Speakers Group at www.TheMorganJamesSpeakersGroup.com.

Shelfie

A **free** eBook edition is available with the purchase of this print book.

CLEARLY PRINT YOUR NAME ABOVE IN UPPER CASE

Instructions to claim your free eBook edition:
1. Download the Shelfie app for Android or iOS
2. Write your name in **UPPER CASE** above
3. Use the Shelfie app to submit a photo
4. Download your eBook to any device

ISBN   978-1-60037-492-0

Published by:

EXPERTS ACADEMY PRESS

an imprint of
Morgan James Publishing, LLC

Cover & Interior Design by:
Rachel Lopez
www.r2cdesign.com

In an effort to support local communities and raise awareness and funds, Morgan James Publishing donates a percentage of all book sales for the life of each book to Habitat for Humanity Peninsula and Greater Williamsburg.

Get involved today, visit
www.MorganJamesBuilds.com

Habitat for Humanity®
Peninsula and
Greater Williamsburg
Building Partner

PRAISE FOR *THE STUDENT LEADERSHIP GUIDE*

"ALL TOO OFTEN, STUDENTS ARE ENCOURAGED to become leaders, without an adequate framework that describes the practice and purpose of leadership... *The Student Leadership Guide* helps fill that void. Drawing on his own experience as a student and a professional, the author guides readers through the six "E"s of leadership—envision, enlist, embody, empower, evaluate, and encourage. With numerous questions for discussion and reflection included, this title would be appropriate as the text for a seminar on leadership, the guide for a leadership retreat, or as suggested reading for any emerging student leader on campus."

—UNIVERSITY BUSINESS MAGAZINE

"*The Student Leadership Guide* does a great job of putting the servant leadership philosophy into everyday language and practice. It is an important resource in Kiwanis International's Key Leader program."

—Lanton L. Lee, *Director of Leadership Education and Development, Kiwanis International*

"*The Student Leadership Guide* is thoughtful, engaging, and full of practical suggestions. Brendon Burchard does an excellent job of weaving together the best of the theoretical literature on leadership with a variety of popular treatments of the subject. His analysis and recommendations revolve around a set of guidelines that are not only useful but also inspiring. Aspiring student leaders as well as experienced ones stand to gain a lot from reading this book, reflecting on its lessons, and putting them into practice in a way that fits the situation and the people in it. This is a guidebook to read, keep and revisit."

—George Cheney, PhD, *author, Values at Work*

"Too often teachers of leadership make the concept too idealistic and, therefore, remote and inaccessible. Burchard has done something very special with The Student Leadership Guide. He has made leadership understandable, accessible, and thoroughly desirable. The six "E"s alone are worth the price of admission. It should be required reading for all students. Cancel that. It should be required reading for all aspiring leaders!"

—BILL TREASURER, *executive leadership coach
and author of Right Risk*

"*The Student Leadership Guide* by Brendon Burchard is an interesting and compelling read from both practical and academic standpoints. This guide does not take a "ten minute manager" approach to the subject; on the contrary, it is well grounded in contemporary theories and philosophies of leadership. As importantly, it takes an interesting and easy-to-read approach to leadership and applies it to situations that university students are very likely to find themselves in. I have already recommended it to several of my students who have expressed interest in the theory and practice of leadership and will gladly do so again."

—SHIV GANESH, PHD, *Communications Instructor,
University of Montana*

"This guide lays out paths toward leadership. It will assist you in understanding that leaders are common people who, with focus and determination, work collectively."

—PAT WILLIAMS, *former U.S. Congressman and
Chairman of the Post-Secondary Education Committee*

"Burchard's book is a good tool for anyone who is serious about trying to make a difference in themselves as well as the lives of others."

—ASSOCIATION OF COLLEGE UNIONS INTERNATIONAL

About the Author

Brendon Burchard, who has been called "the student leader's leader," is founder of The College Success Summit™ (www.CollegeSuccessSummit.com) and an award-winning speaker on student life and leadership.

Brendon has an impressive track record of student *and* corporate leadership experience. In high school he was managing editor for the nation's #1 ranked student newspaper. In college he supervised the toughest dorms on campus, conducted workshops on romantic relationships and communication, and chartered a peer mediation program. In graduate school he taught public speaking courses, worked as a peer counselor, and served as a commissioned facilitator and mediator for his university while maintaining a 4.0 GPA. Brendon holds a MA in organizational communication.

Since graduating, Brendon has served as a leadership development and change management consultant for the world's greatest retailers, including JCPenney, eBay, Best Buy, Nordstrom, Levi's, Gateway, and Walgreens. He has designed a Fortune Global 500 company's leadership and innovation program, cocreated The University of Montana Center for Leadership Development's curriculum, developed a large retailer's senior executive coaching training, created a global nonprofit's youth leadership program, and served on several nonprofit advisory boards. He also founded The College Success Summit™, the nation's premier college readiness and success seminar.

Brendon speaks to thousands of students and professionals each year on leadership, communication and motivation. To meet him, or to book a speech for your next event, visit **www.BrendonBurchard.com.**

PRAISE FOR THE AUTHOR

"IT WAS PURE INSPIRATION having Brendon Burchard as our keynote speaker for our leadership conference. I've never seen a speaker connect with so many students on such a personal level. Our students and staff raved about how much they learned from him, how he inspired them to commit to making changes in their lives, in their relationships, and in their leadership practice."

—JENNIFER CLARK, *Student Leadership Institute, University of Houston, Clear Lake*

"Students rarely have the opportunity to hear such words of inspiration and wisdom. Brendon Burchard radiates a tremendous amount of positive energy, which is contagious! He really amazed the students. Many students commented on how great his sessions were and how they will apply what they learned to be a better leader and a better person."

—FATIMA GOINES, *Office of Student Life and Leadership, Georgia State University*

"Brendon brought an incredible air of excitement and energy to our event. He truly connected with students through his real life experiences and powerful metaphors. He engaged students in their lives and inspired them to take the next step. He proved to them that life and leadership can be fun, passionate, exciting, and fulfilling."

—CAIRN LINDLOFF, *Student Activities and Leadership Development, University of Montana*

"Awesome and amazing! Brendon boiled leadership down to the basics and engaged students in the process of realizing their leadership potential."

—MATT KITCHIE, *Leadership Advisor, Miami University*

TABLE OF CONTENTS

ACKNOWLEDGMENTS

THIS FOURTH EDITION IS LIKE the first—it would not have been possible without the beauty of family and friendship that has embraced and emboldened my life.

Mom and Dad, your supportive and loving presence has been the foundation of all our accomplishments, and, more importantly, the triumphant reminder of our own humanity. In the creation of that magically warm and peaceful place we call home, you introduced us to the wondrous promises of security, love, and family. You have done more for me than I can ever articulate, and I hope to emulate you in my own family in the future. Your love is my life.

David, Bryan, and Helen, I would be lost in this world without you. You are my brothers and sister, my best friends, my images of hope and inspiration, and the constant reminder that I have been blessed by God. You've watched me grow and often led the way. You all make me proud, and I pray I do the same.

Linda Ballew, you embraced me as I was—which was difficult, since I never stood still—and uplifted my hidden talents and ambitions. As a teacher and as a loving human, you have been the inspiration and encouraging force in countless lives. Without you and my family, I wouldn't have begun to grow and become wiser, achieved such motivation and morality, or learned that service to others is what life is all about. For your leadership in the formative years of my life, I will always remember you with love.

I will forever be indebted to the Communication Studies Department at The University of Montana. It is home not only to the most renowned professors in the field, but also to the most supportive and genuine people I've ever met. Wes, thank you for talking me into staying. To the amazing graduate students who helped me through, especially Dan Lair and Bryan Hansen, thank you. And special thanks to George Cheney, my advisor. George, you allowed me to pursue my interests and showed me what service means in the working world. Your unwavering dedication to your students and the field of communication studies will always be remembered and will serve as an example of our true ability to integrate work and passion.

To the numerous coworkers and clients who have believed in me, given me opportunity, and reminded me to be myself: I cannot name you here, but you know who you are. I am thankful for your influence, collaboration, compassion, playfulness, and friendship.

The second edition of this book happened only because of the fire and faith Jean Lange and Adam Standiford reawakened within me one night long ago in Seattle, Washington. Their belief in me and my message of service helped rejuvenate my leadership and speaking career, and I am forever indebted.

This fourth edition marks the launch of my College Success Summit™, the nation's premier college readiness and success seminar. Nearly fifty percent of students who begin college never actually graduate, and we have to do something about it. The Summit is my effort to do just that. I'm uniting 1000-plus students with the nation's best collegiate educators, speakers, entrepreneurs, and leaders so that they can learn how to succeed in college emotionally, socially, academically, financially, and spiritually. Thank you to Jennifer Clark, Erin Fischer, and Jennifer Jacobs for believing in the vision and helping me launch the program. To register to attend, or to learn more about this life-changing seminar, visit us online at **CollegeSuccessSummit.com.**

Finally, to those who have given the greatest service of all: lifelong friendship. To Jason Sorenson, Gwenda Houston, Dave Ries, Adam Standiford, Brandon VandeVan, Erann Brown, Matt and Mark Hiesterman, Dam-on Murdo, Ryan Groepper, Steve Roberts, Jesse Brunner, Andy Breun-inger, Erin Kissock, Brian Simonson, Reed Trontel, Jessica Schwarz, Jeff Buszmann, Dave Smith, Mitch Todd, Jessy Villano, Janine Yaxley, Nick DeDominic, Dana Fetrow, Phil Bernard, Stephan Blendstrup, and Denise DeVault: I couldn't have done it without your enduring reminders not to take myself too seriously. I could write a book on each of your contributions to my life—or at least a successful sitcom. All of you, in ways I'll never quite be able to de-scribe, sparked my passion for life and renewed my sense of adventure, humor, spirit, and purpose. Thanks for sharing stories, lies, and the hot news, not messing up the main line, and trouncing playfully on my overwhelming sense of self. I love you all.

INTRODUCTION

Toward a Leadership Mind-set

"We wait too long."

I could tell this was going to be a trying moment for Aaron, for the both of us. It was rare for him to talk like this, and I knew it was time for me to listen. We were walking our favorite path around the university, surrounded by the beauty of a snow-blanketed winter's evening. Maybe it was the dreamy stillness of the night. Maybe it was that our time in college was coming to an end, and our friendship was about to be separated by thousands of miles. Regardless, we were in an introspective mood, and our words were the only sounds in the unstirring darkness.

"What did I do in college?" said Aaron. "We did have a great time. I met and made the friends of a lifetime. But what did I really accomplish? I didn't care or excel much in my classes, I didn't have a job but for one year, and I didn't even join any clubs."

His voice was subdued, and I worried that he was getting down on himself. "You don't have to have done those things to—"

"I know, Brendon—just wait a minute." He paused, turned away from me, and stared longingly into a field of powder-capped pines. "The thing is…I didn't have or serve any purpose here. You don't know how people talk about you. When you leave a room, we talk about all the things you've done. We talk about all the people you've lifted up. People don't do that with me."

Maybe for the first time in our friendship, I didn't know what to say.

"My fear now is that I'm going to be an eighty-year-old man on a rocking chair, on the porch of some cabin, looking back at my life and saying, 'I wish I woulda, shoulda.' You know, I wanted to do a lot of things when I came here, but I just didn't get around to it. I wanted to be strong; I wanted to be a leader. But I never got off the ground—maybe because I didn't know how, or didn't know I could. But now I'm leaving this university in a semester, and I haven't done the things I dreamed of doing." We had stopped walking, and he looked toward the flickering yellow glow of the avenue leading to his house. "We just wait too long to chase our dreams, as if college is an excuse to suspend life. We wait too long, Brendon, and that's why no one will remember me."

He didn't say another word and walked what must have been a long journey home.

I thought for a long time about what Aaron said, and realized he was the voice of many students. I talked to him days later, and he told me of the clubs he wished he had started, the work environments he wished he had improved, and the leadership roles he wished he had taken. He regretted not having more purpose, not serving others, not living life, and not leaving a legacy. And as if hearing a whisper in my head, I remembered a quote that spoke to his words and feelings. It was something I had first read in a leadership book and then, years later, read again in another. From the great playwright George Bernard Shaw, it was in Steven Covey's *Principle-Centered Leadership* and Bennis and Goldsmith's *Learning to Lead*. I typed it, brought it to Aaron, and watched him carry it during our last semester of college as he went about changing his life—and leaving the legacy he had come so close to letting slip away. The quote, from Shaw's *Man and Superman,* helped Aaron re-unite with his ambition to live, contribute, and lead:

> This is the true joy in life, the being used for a purpose recognized by yourself as a mighty one; the being a force of nature instead of a feverish selfish little clod of ailments and grievances complaining that the world will not devote itself to making you happy. I am of the opinion that my life belongs to the whole community and as I live it is my privilege—my *privilege* to do for it whatever I can. I want to thoroughly be used up when I die, for the harder I work the more I live. I rejoice in life for its own sake. Life is no "brief candle" to me. It is a sort of splendid torch which I have got hold of for the moment, and I want to make it burn as brightly as possible before handing it on to future generations.

A New Beginning Through Leadership

In *The Student's Leadership Guide* you will find a new beginning, much as Aaron did. He wanted to serve a greater purpose, to contribute, to be remembered, to live a life of his own design, and to leave his community better than he found it. You can do this through leadership. I am not saying leadership is the only way. I am not suggesting that leadership always leads to these results. Nor am I glorifying leadership as the cure-all for a "feverish" life.

What I am proposing, however, is that leadership provides us with unique and powerful challenges to grow and contribute. Leadership makes us aim our efforts, give of ourselves, and create meaningful relationships and changes. Through this process, I believe we become stronger. We can accomplish Aaron's goals. We can, in a very real and authentic way, leave a lasting legacy through leadership. This guide's intent is to help you understand and practice leadership to do just that.

By reading this book, you will be reunited with many of your signature strengths and ambitions to lead. You will likely report a renewed desire to contribute to your university or the greater community simply by learning to lead. I say this only because of the extraordinary feedback I received from the first two editions of this book.

Though initially published for the students at The University of Montana's Center for Leadership Development, the *Guide* found a surprising following through word of mouth and has ultimately touched many students' lives. Since its first publication in May 2001, I have received hundreds of e-mails from students who have taken on greater leadership positions using the information you will find ahead. People have told me they became stronger, wiser, more collaborative, and more focused on helping others. I believe that you can do the same.

Students are the most ambitious, creative, and idealistic group of people I know. You are inspired and motivated and hopeful. You look at society and its challenges through a fresh perspective. You hope to do work that benefits the masses and the world itself. You dream big and get caught up in conversations that stir you. You are collaborative and hope to pursue shared purposes and help others grow in the process. This guide aims to help you channel all these myriad strengths in order to become the best leaders possible.

The approach that lies ahead may surprise you. These pages may not contain exactly what you thought you'd get from a book with "student" in the title. I have done my best to provide an approach and framework to leadership that is relatively context free. That is, this is not specifically a book on leadership for student government. It is not a leadership book just for student volunteers, or fraternities or sororities. Or honor societies, community programs, or classroom project teams. This book is not aimed at any specific student group. Rather, it is focused on helping you become a leader regardless of your position, title, role, or membership. The powerful framework that lies in the pages ahead will be adaptable to any situation you find yourself in. I've seen the framework succeed in both the classroom and the boardroom. You will have to judge whether it is useful to you and your purposes. For in the end, leadership is about fitting the right approach to the right context, with the right people involved, to get the right things done.

So you won't find here example after example of students leading in particular contexts, or verbose, heartwarming stories of leaders changing the world. I'll leave that to *Chicken Soup*. Instead, what you will find ahead are the nuts and bolts of this thing called leadership. It is not applied to any specific context, so that you can apply it to your own.

Leadership is something you will be called to do. Great economic, social, and global issues face us, and leaders will help craft significant dialogue, visions, and changes to address them. There's a lot of work involved in building a better society. You have probably already found causes that are important to you and your communities. You have probably seen injustice, greed, helplessness, broken bureaucracies, and corruption. You may also have seen inspiring programs and efforts meant to address our most difficult challenges. I have no doubt that you have wanted to become involved and make significant changes in the way the world lives and works.

Unfortunately, though, many of us never *lead* those changes. We want change—in our friends, our communities, our world, and ourselves—but how often do we, as students, craft it? Instead we create prisons in our minds that prevent us from taking leadership roles to effect the changes we want. These prisons are built by the suspicions that we are alone, have no power, lack capabilities and experience, are not deserving or worthy, and that others are preventing us from succeeding. We then fall into the traditional roles of helpless, unconnected members of our universities and society, rather than filling the innovative roles as architects of our age.

I believe that we as students fail to become the architects, the leaders, of the future for two reasons. First is the old demon fear. We can view it as an acronym, FEAR: fear of *failure, embarrassment, anxiety, and rejection.* These emotions are particularly prominent in the student age range. They are the emotions that paralyze, demoralize, and victimize. They cause us to stop our efforts, to feel weakened, and to blame others for the conditions we find ourselves in. I don't pretend to know how to banish these emotions. I do know, however, that student leaders are more apt to overcome the demons of doubt associated with these emotions if they develop the personal strength that comes from leading their fellow students in pursuit of something important.

Second, we fail to become leaders because we lack the twin forces of ambition *and* initiative, the essential traits of leaders.[1] How can that be? Certainly, visitors to university campuses often report that they leave feeling rejuvenated and inspired by the power of the student body's ambition and idealism. This is because we believe we can change the world with dramatic flare and innovative, status quo–challenging thought. Our hopes and dreams are not tied to this moment in time—we see the future because we *are* the future. Our diverse educational experience exposes us to a great range of issues and opportunities, and our conversations are abuzz with them. As a professor once told me, "Students absolutely *breathe* ambition." So I am certainly not saying we lack ambition.

Though our force of ambition is unparalleled, our challenge is that we often fail to couple this ambition with the force of initiative. A student body president once told me, "Our ambition is equaled only by our apathy." But I don't think apathy is the problem. Apathy is lumped together with "laziness" or a "lack of interest" or of concern for the important matters of the day. I would challenge anyone who says that students are lazy. We just get caught up in multiple causes, classes, and communities. Our lives are in a whirlpool of change, and it is challenging enough to stay afloat as we attempt our first shot at independence, higher education, and changing living conditions and social situations. I also believe that students are extremely concerned about the issues of the day, particularly their own. The important causes of the day, though, can often take a backseat to our struggle to keep our values in check, our dreams alive, and our wallets full.

That said, we still struggle to put our convictions into practice. We *want,* but we don't *be* or *do.* We are extremely concerned, but we don't always take action. This is our greatest challenge as students: to couple the forces of our ambition with the force of meaningful initiative.

If you find a cause you believe in, don't shelve it. Don't wait until you finish this semester to do something. Don't wait until you finish the internship, or get voted into the senate, or get inspired by a professor or a friend. If you do, you are cheating more than the cause you believe in—you are cheating yourself. If you back away from those issues that raise gut-level emotions and concerns, then you back away from your authentic self.

Indeed, if we don't act on what we believe, we succumb to the "Jonah complex." The famed psychologist Dr. Abraham Maslow used the complex "to describe a documented psychological group of symptoms found in people who run away from their real calling in life."[2] You don't have to figure out your calling right now, but you'd better listen to your passions and act on them. Every time you feel compelled to act but fail to do so out of fear; every time you want to voice an opinion but are gagged by your own inner censor; every time you turn from your responsibilities and signature strengths—these are the times you have begun to fail your calling. Worse yet, you have begun to fail your greatest calling as a human being: to leave the world better than you found it.

As students, luckily, we find ourselves in unique positions that *demand* that we overcome a lack of initiative. We run into old ideas that no longer work, new programs being built, people seeking guidance, and new causes needing support. We might find red tape that needs shredding, corruption that needs exposure, or anger that needs temperance. In so many ways, student life has a refreshing way of defeating our tendencies to hide within ourselves and not take important actions.

I guarantee that at some point you'll find yourself in a crisis situation, on the apex of change, or just in one of those situations where everyone is looking to you for answers. And if you listen closely enough, you will hear, amid the questions and uncertainty, the gentle stirrings of the leader inside you. You will take initiative; you will act; you will walk from your fear and turn conviction to conduct.

The leader is there. No contemporary leadership theorist believes that leadership lies within only a select few. You don't have to have a high-powered job, be strong, rich, tall, or good looking, or have any other special trait that was once paired with leadership.[3] You have the personal power to become a great leader. Leadership abilities reside in all of us and will be drawn up from our deepest being in order to help others.

Leadership is first a journey inward. As in Oz, everything you want to be, you already are. Sometimes it just takes a little challenge and adventure to discover yourself. It's through the reflective and participative processes of leadership that you can begin to find your ambitions and values. It's through the relationships and purposes of leadership that you can achieve a higher sense of self through helping others to do exactly the same. This guide, then, can be as much about personal development as it is about leadership.

Reading this book will feel like a new beginning for you. It will help you understand this thing called leadership. It will help crystallize your ambition into a vision. And most importantly, it will help you take initiative and measurable, responsible steps toward becoming a leader.

Why We Need Leaders Now

Without an understanding of leadership, students are unable to become effective agents of positive change in their own lives, in the organizations they work in, and in their greater communities.

We live in an amazing time of technological innovation, societal shifting, and globalization that has left us, ironically, at once dependent and disconnected. Unfortunately, according to the prominent politician and leadership theorist John Gardner, "We give every appearance of sleepwalking through a dangerous passage of history."[4] We can't continue to avoid the important issues of the day. We can't turn the other way. We can't walk past those in need. We simply can't avoid taking the lead in our lives and helping society to grow stronger.

As First Lady Abigail Adams said, "Great necessities call forth great leaders."[5] And at no other time are leaders being called so strongly. Leaders are needed to help navigate today's turbulent waters and guide us to higher grounds. Robert Greenleaf, advocate of "servant leadership," notes,

> The urgent problems of our day—the disposition to venture into immoral and senseless wars, destruction of the environment, poverty, alienation, discrimination, overpopulation—exist because of human failures, individual failures, one-person-at-a-time, one-action-at-a-time failures.[6]

It will be leaders, one-by-one, whose actions, one at a time, will help society address its urgent problems. Many of these problems come from dominant cultural values and beliefs. So many of us are still marching to the calls of "achieve, look good, don't fail, make money, become powerful, be the champion, crush the competition." Possibly because of this, the prominent psychologist James Hillman commented, "Character died in the twentieth century."[7] Indeed, our society's focus on individualism has eroded our character as a nation. Our intense focus on serving ourselves, rather than the common good, may be the most urgent problem of our day.

But there is a slow, steady shift away from such self-serving ideals. The calls to individualism are being countered by the whispers of higher ideals to "contribute, grow by trying, embrace and serve others, be a supporter, give others the stage." Suddenly, we are hearing the chants of *significance* rise above the chants of *success.*

We have made headway and accomplished great feats in the past century. At no other time in history, though, has Thoreau's admonition rung so true: "The mass of men lead lives of quiet desperation." And now the quiet desperation has found a voice and chorused into a thunderous cry for help. Simply looking through the morning paper, we see these cries evidenced in stories of corruption, alienation, depression, cynicism, and hopelessness. And rather than attempt to solve these crises by taking individual responsibility and embracing the ideals of helping others, our society resorts to drug prescriptions and engages in useless finger pointing.

Ultimately, it will fall on the shoulders of our society's leaders to help solve these problems. Leadership is not the cure of all ills, but it can help. We must start somewhere, and that somewhere can be a place where we assume leadership roles to help others achieve their aspirations tied to the common good—a place where we serve mutual visions that help others achieve a higher sense of self. We can, person by person and leader by leader, turn the cries of alienation, heartache, and fear into the laughter and song of hope and renewal.

WHAT LEADERSHIP MEANS TO YOU

I shouldn't have been able to walk away from a car wreck ten years ago. I was in a drunk-driving accident in which our car was completely destroyed after flipping numerous times at eighty miles an hour. The driver nearly had his head taken off and was later diagnosed with signs of brain injury. I was injured as well, but I focus more on the lessons that endured from the wreck than on the temporary injuries. I have never known why I survived, but I have come to the conclusion that there was another plan for me.

So many of us are blinded by the assumption that to-morrow is promised and that we'll have time to accomplish our dreams next year. Some of us, though, are blessed to realize that tomorrow may not come and that we'd best get busy living. Some of us, like Aaron, are confronted with leaving an environment and realize that we may not be leaving the legacy we had dreamed of.

Your time to become a leader, to take hold of your dreams and rein them in, is now. It's time to awaken your ambitions from slumber and take the first steps to achieving a destiny that you've constructed. I was a peer counselor for four years in college, and now I play a coaching role to both students and professionals. One thought has been at the center of my work: we need to have a dream—a vision of our ideal inner and outer world—and we have to take responsible measures to move to ward its fulfillment. This is the stuff of personal leadership.

When I've told people this in the past, they've stared at me with undirected inspiration—they're excited about becoming causal agents in their lives but have no idea how to begin. They like the idea of having a dream and taking action. They ask me how, and I tell them they can start through leadership. They ask me, "Where do I begin," and I answer, "With leadership." I tell them that leadership roles allow us to define ourselves and our vision, work with others to hone that vision, and collectively seek important purposes beyond ourselves. I tell them that leadership reminds us to take responsible actions to fulfill our dreams and build our character.

And then something peculiar happens. They keep staring at me, still floundering for the answer, awash in the ambiguity of the word "leadership." I regularly find people willing to accept that assuming leadership, for themselves and others, can help them grow stronger and contribute to their world. These same people, though, have little or no idea what leadership is, or at least they cannot articulate it.

I understand that asking others about leadership is a little unfair. Leadership has been likened to the abominable snowman—you see the tracks but never the thing itself. For those who want to grasp leadership and its promise to stir the soul and chase down our dreams, though, the question must be asked.

So now I ask you, "What is leadership?" In one sentence, tell me what leadership means to you. Answer the question right now. Don't stew on it too long; answer this moment: what is leadership?

After speaking to thousands of people one on one, in small groups, and in large auditoriums, I find time and time again that people cannot answer the question. From university students to corporate professionals, I have found very few who could define the term for themselves.

At the same time, if I ask, "What is a leader?" or "What are the traits of leaders?" people can shoot the answer out immediately with a plethora of descriptors. The same goes for "What do leaders do?" This is insightful in many ways. Mostly it tells us that people can generally define what a leader is and does, but can't exactly define leadership itself. This is a problem.

To explain, let me draw an analogy. Think of the words "running" and "runner." We can say that a runner is fast, flexible, focused, healthy, and full of endurance. We can say that a runner values healthy eating habits, an active training schedule, and improvement in her performance. We can say such descriptors until we are blue in the face, and we will still not come away with a *workable understanding* of what a runner is. It is impossible to explain it without explaining the action term "running." Once we define "running," though, we are much more effective explaining "runner"— someone who is consistently engaged in running. Similarly, we may be sprinting ahead to explain "leader" ("runner") before understanding "leadership" ("running").

My guess is that you've picked up this book in hopes of discovering more about leadership, clarifying your own philosophies, and learning how to hone them in practice. This can't happen, though, until you've reached inside, looking for deeper meanings and truths. There is no singular answer to the question "What is leadership?" Rather, there are as many definitions of "leadership" as there are people who study it.[8]

If you don't begin with some concept of what leadership is, this guide will be of little benefit to you. For in the end it will be a culmination of your genius and actions, hopefully coupled with a few concepts from this guide, which help you become a leader. So you must answer, "What is leadership?"

To help others address this daunting question, I often ask a set of questions to guide them to a more definitive answer. These questions are posed in the next few pages. Leadership is a mystical thing to many, esoteric and ungraspable. As John Gardner reminds us in *On Leadership,* "The first step is not action; the first step is understanding. The first question is how to think about leadership."[9] *Only through defining leadership will you be able to understand it. And only through understanding it will you ever be able to practice it.* That is why you must take significant time to answer the following questions.

Don't be the typical reader and breeze over these questions, believing them to be trite and irrelevant. These questions will help you understand the magic of leadership in your life and, hopefully, inspire you to reciprocate. The questions are easy and short; your answers shouldn't be. Not if you really want to get this leadership stuff. Not if you are really going to take on leadership roles.

So lock your door now. Unplug the phone and computer. Relax and really think about these questions. They will help you and may inspire the boldness of heart it will take for you to complete this guide. Grab your pen. Take time filling out the answer to each question, attempting to choose the most inspiring and moving examples you can.

Make this an effort that counts, and your understanding of the dream of leadership may begin to form the reality of tomorrow.

Leadership Questions

1. What do you think leadership is? Narrow it down to four sentences or less.

2. Who was a memorable leader in your life?

3. What were some of that leader's personal characteristics?

4. What did this person do for the people he was leading?

5. How did she make you or her followers feel?

6. How did this leader motivate you or other followers?

7. How do you feel about that leader now?

8. What kind of leader would you like to be?

PRINCIPLES OF LEADERSHIP

Understanding the role and function of leadership is the single most important intellectual task of this generation, and leading is the most needed skill.

—G.W. FAIRHOLM, *Perspectives on Leadership*

Leadership by itself will not change the world. It does have the potential to change people, though, by helping them achieve a higher purpose through serving and guiding others. As you spent some time answering the questions above, I imagine you felt a heartwarming, perhaps inspiring presence in the room. The presence was the spirit of the leader you wrote about and his or her actions, and the leader within you aspiring to come out. What you wrote about was leadership in your own terms. The rest of this guide will be a journey for you, with many concepts to consider, but these will essentially have to be checked against your experiences, philosophies, values, and, ultimately, your understanding of this thing called leadership.

I have a guiding philosophy about leadership, based on three principles developed from intensive research, a questioning mind-set, and applied practice in leadership roles over the past ten years. It's important to know my mind-set, because it frames the definition of leadership that I'll describe shortly. I believe that the well-grounded roots of these three principles strengthen the process of leadership described in this guide.

Principle 1: Leadership is a collective, not a singular, activity.

In *Leadership Without Easy Answers,* Ronald Heifetz noted, "The myth of leadership is the myth of the lone warrior: the solitary individual whose heroism and brilliance enable him to lead the way."[10] Unfortunately, this myth has pierced the American consciousness. We look to the lone warrior and give over our fate into his hands. We shed our responsibilities and fail to be accountable, because "the leader will take care of us." This lone warrior, this commander of our fate, becomes our projection of hope and life. And if the commander should lose the battle, we cast our stones at him, all the while forgetting that we did not step onto the battlefield ourselves.

Slowly, society is moving away from this myth of one heroic leader who is in charge of our fate. We are learning that we must be involved in defining the vision, we must help plan the strategy, we must fight the fight, we must win our victories with our own efforts, because we are all in this together. "Followers" have as much influence in leadership as leaders.[11] In his landmark book entitled *Leadership*, James MacGregor Burns said, "Leaders and followers are engaged in a common enterprise; they are dependent on each other, their fortunes rise and fall together."[12]

We are approaching a wondrous time when society will not look to a sole individual to command; it will look to many to collaborate. It will see followers as active in the leadership process, rather than as passive people who are merely having something done to them by leaders.[13] We will move from the word "followers" to the word "collaborators." We will no longer look to singular commanders, but rather to communities of shared responsibility and accountability. Communities that we have shaped, encouraged, and emboldened with common values, principles, and aspirations.

As you will see when you read ahead, this guide is centered in the principle of you working with others, not as a commander but as a leader. It is my hope that you will feel empowered and educated after finishing this guide and, thus, more able to help build the community of leadership.

Principle 2: Leadership is not management.

As students we tend to believe that leadership is the same as management. Many of the "leaders" in our lives were those who employed or managed us, and we have been taught for years that leadership is good management.[14] If you get ten people in a room and ask who their leaders are, eight of them will mention a manager at work. This is a disturbing result of how generalized the words "leader" and "leadership" have become. A manager is not necessarily a leader, and a leader is not necessarily a manager. This distinction is not mere wordplay but a vital differentiation in philosophy, objectives, means, and values. Understanding this distinction will also be vital to your success as a leader.

Despite many of our basic social values about hierarchy, you can be a leader regardless of your position. Mahatma Gandhi didn't have formal powers as a supervisor or manager. Being "boss" does not in itself make a person a leader. In fact, I feel that the belief that one has to hold a high position, whether in society, organization, family, or community, in order to assume leadership is terribly disempowering. Embracing this belief, we begin to think of ourselves as helpless. We begin to think that only those who are "insiders" or "connected" have the power to affect their environment.

The promise, though, is that "outsiders" and "underlings" are the likeliest people to change paradigms, often because those of influence in the current paradigm are stuck in their old patterns.[15] So if you fall prey to the idea that you can assume leadership only with positional power, it's time to for you to change your mind-set.

Understanding this, leadership must be separated from management.[16] Leadership and management are two separate and distinct *roles*, though managers and leaders can be the same *people*.[17]

Let me give you a better picture of the difference between leadership and management by looking at three generalized areas: authority, status quo, and people.

First, leaders' *authority*, if given to them by collaborators, stems from influence. You influence others via your knowledge, skills, character, abilities, personality, and your relationships with them. If others deem you worthy and credible, they will grant you authority and, hopefully, respect and collaboration. Leaders' authority is maintained through transformational influence—the empowerment of collaborators.

Managers' authority, on the other hand, rests in contractual agreements and formal, hierarchically arranged positions. Managers' authority is granted by their position and the power that it grants them. Managers maintain authority through transactional influence—rewards and sanctions that result in compliance.[18] You've probably seen the difference between the two in your work experience. You did something for a manager because you felt you had to; otherwise you'd get fired or reprimanded. Alternatively, you've done something for a leader because you respected, trusted, and shared mutual purposes with her or him.

Second, leaders seek to change and improve the status quo through envisioning the future. Leaders look at the long-term possibilities and objectives, seeking to adapt and innovate. They are not known for doing things the "same old way." Instead of merely "doing things right," they "do the right things." They are focused on making significant changes and are often innovative in the way they implement those changes. Leaders operate in "tomorrow" and in the renewal of ideas, values, and organizations. They are visionary change agents.[19]

Managers seek to maintain standards. They operate in "today" by seeking to make it "work right." They work with the day-to-day operations and distributions of resources, hoping to become more efficient and to better control systems, procedures, and policies. Often they look to tomorrow only to make sure they are meeting predefined goals. They are controllers who implement ideas.

Finally, leaders and managers are further differentiated by the way they work with their people. Leaders work with *col-*

laborators in pursuit of *mutual* purposes. They seek to help their people grow stronger through encouraging flexibility, creativity, and innovation. They *inspire* their people and raise them to "higher standards of motivation and morality."[20] They coach, mentor, and counsel collaborators in hopes of *serving* them and a greater vision. They form close relationships with their collaborators and are *caregivers*. In other words, they *earn* their collaborators' trust and commitment.

Managers work with *subordinates* in pursuit of *top-down* objectives. They seek to help their organization work in the present through controlling work efforts in standardized ways. They *direct* their people and occasionally raise them to higher performance against preset benchmarks. They mentor subordinates in hopes of managing their performance. They distance themselves from subordinates in order not to "cross the lines" of work and personal lives, which would make them *caretakers*. Managers are *assigned* their subordinates.

These are broad generalizations, and again I remind you that managers and leaders have different roles, though they may be the same people. While I paint these differences with such generalizations, there is no doubt a difference between the roles of managers and leaders. You've worked with both, and you've felt the difference.

With these distinctions in mind, you must see that leadership is not one person directing others or doing something to others so that they will do what he wants them to do. That is management, headship, coercion, authority wielding. Leadership is based on influence and the pursuit of mutual purposes. This principle is grounded in a new paradigm of leadership that moves away from the desire to direct, control, and manipulate and toward influential acts of encouragement, empowerment, support, facilitation, and service.

Principle 3: Leadership is rooted in service.

If you seek enlightenment for yourself simply to enhance yourself and your position, you miss the purpose; if you seek enlightenment for yourself to enable you to serve others, you are with purpose.

—Dalai Lama

If someone were to ask me what leadership theories I believe and practice, I would tell them it is a culmination of Robert Greenleaf's ideas of servant leadership and James MacGregor Burns's transformational leadership. The two ideas are very similar, and anyone would greatly benefit from reading Greenleaf's books Servant Leadership, The Servant as Leader, and On Becoming a Servant Leader, and Burns's book Leadership. Both theories have a common thread running through them: that service is the root of leadership. The idea of service is explicit in Greenleaf's writings and implicit in Burns's. Indeed, transformational leadership is all about serving collaborators by helping transform them into better individuals.

To better understand the idea of service in leadership, let me first discuss (1) what servant leadership is about, and (2) what and who is served in this type of leadership.

Servant leadership puts others first—collaborators, employees, customers, community—in hopes of promoting a sense of community and shared power in decision making.[21] Greenleaf writes,

> It begins with the natural feeling that one wants to serve, to serve first. Then conscious choice brings one to aspire to lead. The difference manifests itself in the care taken by the servant—first to make sure that other people's highest priority needs are served. The best test is: Do those served grow as persons; do they, while being served, become healthier, wiser, freer, more autonomous, more likely themselves to become servants?

Larry Spears, editor of *Insights on Leadership*, further explains,

> As we near the end of the twentieth century, we are beginning to see that traditional, autocratic, and hierarchical modes of leadership are yielding to a newer model—one based on teamwork and community, one that seeks to involve others in decision making, one strongly based in ethical and caring behavior, and one that is attempting to enhance the personal growth of workers [collaborators] while improving the caring and quality of our many institutions [communities]. This emerging approach to leadership and service is called *servant-leadership*.[22]

Servant leadership reminds us that leaders are first people who serve the needs of others. Indeed, if collaborators didn't believe that their leaders were serving them, they would walk away. This principle should be paramount in all your thoughts about leadership. You, as a leader, have the obligation to serve others. As Greenleaf notes, "The choices any of us can make, no matter how intolerable our lot, is to use the freedom and resources we possess to make others' lives more significant."[23] Servant leaders find out what other people need and what they aspire to achieve, and help them to do so. Servant leaders consistently and honestly ask themselves and collaborators, "How can I help?"

Servant leaders believe that one person can make a difference and that their own identities and behavior are geared toward serving others. Greenleaf also believes that leaders must live what they preach, and focus on who they really are, not what they do. In this sense, servant leaders don't seek to use the latest how-to fads; they don't seek to reduce leadership to a checklist. Instead they focus on becoming people of integrity and accountability. Peter Drucker recalls that when a seminar participant approached Greenleaf and asked, "What do I do?" Greenleaf immediately answered, "That comes later. First, what do you want to be?"[24] Similarly, Frances Hesselbein, former CEO of the Girl Scouts of America and chair of the Drucker Foundation, says, "Leadership is a matter of how to be, not how to do it." Being a servant to your collaborators is the "how to be" of leadership. We will return to this point later as we discuss the framework for leadership. For ultimately, the framework is heavily grounded in this principle.

Servant leaders seek to help others grow and become healthier, wiser, and more autonomous by asking, "How can I help?" and embodying the ideals of responsibility and accountability. Servant leadership, in effect, dedicates service for two things: service for a vision and service to collaborators.

Service for a Vision

Leadership is about coming together and seeking important ends, ideals, changes, and values. If there were not something that leaders and collaborators hoped to achieve, they would never come together under this thing we call leadership. Think of the great leaders of history, and you immediately think of their vision: George Washington and democracy, Martin Luther King Jr. and civil rights, Mother Theresa and service to the world's needy.

You enlist others to help you achieve something important. That vision, and the dedicated pursuit of its attainment, is what leadership is all about. Indeed, possibly the most important factor in leadership is the answer to the question "What are we here to do?"

Service to Collaborators

Leadership is a relationship,[25] and servant leadership recognizes the absolute necessity of enhancing and transforming the members of that relationship. In recognizing this, service to collaborators becomes the second main factor in servant leadership. Collaborators are "served" by servant leaders through the transforming effect of helping them grow, become wiser, healthier, freer, and more autonomous. In this sense, serving collaborators closely parallels Burns's transformational leadership.

In *Leadership for the Twenty-First Century*, Joseph Rost writes, "Leadership is about transformation."[26] Transformational leadership, according to its founder, James Mac-Gregor Burns, occurs when people "*engage* with others in such a way that leaders and followers raise one another to higher levels of motivation and morality."[27] Citing Mahatma Gandhi as an example, Burns reminds us that leadership "becomes *moral* in that it raises the level of human conduct and ethical aspiration of both the leader and the led, and thus it has a transforming effect on both."[28]

Transformational leadership's grandest statement is that it fuses the purposes of leaders and collaborators together. Burns sees that leaders and followers together make leadership happen, and in doing so, they become better people He feels this potential for transforming people through leadership so strongly, he ends his book with this sentence: "That people can be lifted *into* their better selves is the secret of transforming leadership and the moral and practical theme of this work."[29]

When people identify their ideal type of leadership, transformational leadership is most often described.[30] You've probably been influenced by a transformational leader who made you want to achieve your best and helped you do it in a way that made you a better person. Transformational leadership, then, is a way for leaders to provide a *service* to their collaborators. By helping people reach "higher levels of motivation and morality," leadership provides a service to them. That is why I emphasize that leadership is rooted in service, and advocate servant leadership as the theme throughout this guide.

Because servant leadership is about service to collaborators through transformational leadership, I don't believe there is such a thing as a "bad" leader. For example, many people would argue that Hitler was a leader. But coming from a transformational leadership viewpoint that insists that leaders serve their collaborators, he cannot be considered one. I doubt that many would call him a person who raised others to "higher levels of morality." You cannot be moral if you do immoral things to others. Further, since Burns tells us, "transformational leadership is more concerned with end-values such as liberty, justice, equality,"[31] Hitler fails here, too, to qualify as a leader. He certainly didn't champion liberty or equality. He was a tyrant and a dictator—an effective communicator, an excellent organizer, and a master motivator, true—but *not* a leader.

Similarly, if someone "guides" or inspires you to steal a car and kill someone, I wouldn't call him or her a leader.

Similarly, if a manager leads you to do something that ultimately wipes out an employee pension fund, I wouldn't call that manager a leader. Under the ideals of servant leadership, collaborators must become wiser and healthier, and I doubt that they can do it by stealing a car or hurting or impoverishing someone. Ethics and morals are a large part of servant leadership, so if someone guides you to be immoral, unethical, or unjust, I would *never* call that person a leader.

Servant leaders are true leaders. As a matter of fact, I don't see any appreciable distinction between true leaders and other kinds. You don't say, "This is a *true* bicycle"; it is or it isn't a bicycle. Likewise, a person is or isn't a leader. If a person is not leading, she or he is doing something else. In the following section you'll see how I define a leader. For now, it's important to realize that because service to collaborators (and thus, transformation) is at the heart of my concept of leadership, I believe that if, by guiding you to do something immoral or unethical, someone works to prevent you from being your best, that person is not a leader, no matter how visionary, charismatic, or enlightened he or she may be.

Leaders serve others rather than looking to be served; they focus on giving over receiving.[32] Servant leaders hope to attain important ends and, at the same time, transform their collaborators so that they are likelier to grow as persons, become healthier, wiser, freer, more autonomous, and likelier to become servants themselves. This type of reasoning led Gardner, in *On Leadership,* to point out,

> Perhaps the most promising trend in our thinking about leadership is the growing conviction that the purposes of the group are best served when the leader helps followers to develop their own initiative, strengthens them in the use of their own judgment, enables them to grow, and to become better contributors."[33]

I believe that servant leadership is the most enduring, powerful, and realistic philosophy of leadership today and will help us realize the worldwide benefits of service to our homes, workplaces, and greater communities as we begin the new millennium.

CHAPTER ONE

THE SEARCH FOR "LEADERSHIP"

I've been withholding something from you for some time now. Hoping that you would begin to form an idea of leadership through the previous section, I purposely left out a discussion of exactly what I believe "leadership" is. I've told you the principles guiding leadership in this text, but I haven't given you a definition. Before I do, it's helpful to look at what we call a leader.

First, a leader is *not* simply someone with specific traits. Just because you may have traits common to leaders, such as self-confidence, integrity, strong cognitive abilities, and an in-depth knowledge of your subject,[34] does not automatically qualify you as a leader. You can be completely trustworthy, inspiring, and possessed of amazing expertise, but you still may not be a leader.[35] Although having these traits may enhance the perception that you have the ability to lead,[36] you can have all these traits and be in a room alone.

Further, a leader is *not* simply someone who displays specific behaviors. Just because you focus on getting tasks and goals accomplished, seek to maintain group and interpersonal functions, and make lots of decisions, you do not automatically qualify as a leader. You can do all these things and be a manager, but not necessarily a leader. If you can accomplish goals and get people to do things, that in itself doesn't make you a leader.

DEFINING LEADERSHIP

So what *is* a leader? Many theorists argue for a definition of leaders as "those who consistently contribute certain kinds of acts to leadership processes," and go on to state that "the only sure means of identifying leaders is through the analysis of leadership processes."[37] Drawing from these statements, and for the purposes of this book, a leader will be defined as *a person engaged in, and who intends to consistently engage in, the leadership process.*

From that statement, we must assume that *leadership is a process.* If you think about it, for leadership to occur, a process must take place wherein leaders and collaborators somehow come together, agree to do something, work with one another, and take actions to do what they have agreed on.

Understanding this, leadership is *the process of leaders and collaborators coming together through an influence relationship and seeking envisioned changes that reflect their mutual purposes.*

This definition is an extension of Joseph Rost's *Leadership for the Twenty-First Century.* He defines leadership as "an influence relationship among leaders and followers who intend real changes that reflect their mutual purpose."[38] (Rost later stopped using the term "followers" and began using the term "collaborators," for the same reasons I discussed earlier.)[39] This book makes two departures from Rost's definition: (1) by moving from leadership as a *relationship* to leadership as a *process,* and (2) by speaking not of *leaders and followers* who *intend* real changes, but of *collaborators* who are *actively seeking* envisioned changes. These are not merely semantic changes, but meaningful distinctions that

I will draw out as I discuss each important component of the definition below.

Leadership is a Process.

People don't just randomly become leaders or collaborators. And worthwhile purposes are not fulfilled by little, halfhearted efforts. A process occurs in which the leader-collaborator relationship is created, maintained, negotiated, strengthened, or ended. A process also occurs wherein leaders and collaborators envision changes and actively seek to accomplish them.

These ideas can help deconstruct the idea that leadership is simply a "relationship." A relationship is a connection between people. And while there is certainly a very special relationship between leaders and collaborators that sets leadership apart from other relationships, leadership is not just the relationship. Leadership theorists have struggled for decades to understand how leaders can strike the right balance between task and relationship. They have done so because both components are involved in leadership: a relationship is being formed, and tasks are getting done. By seeing leadership as just a relationship, we write off the idea that something is getting done, that a process is happening, both inside and outside the relationship, to achieve important purposes.

Leadership is a process, in which (1) an influence relationship is created and maintained between leaders and collaborators, (2) the leaders and collaborators decide what constitutes real change and what reflects their mutual purposes, (3) they seek to create those changes, and (4) they adapt to redefine or ultimately achieve those purposes.

Leaders and Collaborators are in an Influence Relationship.

As we have seen, there is a unique relationship between leaders and followers. Both influence each other throughout the leadership process; leaders are not just doing something to passive followers. An influence relationship means that behaviors of either party are not coercive or based on power *over* another person (power wielding). Rather, the relationship is based on power *with* others, formed by collaboration and noncoercive persuasion. This point is important because it shows that collaborators do not *have* to do what leaders suggest, but must *want* to because they have helped shape those suggestions and believe they are desirable.

Further, an influence relationship means that the leader and collaborators mutually influence one another. There is two-way communication. Perspectives from all parties are heard, respected, and considered in decision-making processes. Collaborators have the ability to say no, to choose appropriate strategies and purposes, and to shape decisions that influence their world.

As leaders, we must constantly remind ourselves that we are in a *relationship* with people, not in a *hierarchy*. We are in a community or family, not an organizational flow chart. We are in a relationship based on mutual needs and interests,[40] not on self-interest.

Leaders and Collaborators are Seeking Changes.

Leaders and collaborators do more than just *intend* real changes. They are doing something to *create* those changes.

"Seeking" means they are actively pursuing changes. They don't have to accomplish them; they just have to engage in behavior, right now, that attempts to accomplish changes. The seeking happens in the present tense, which is important. Leaders and collaborators are not merely intending or hoping to seek change. If they only wish, leadership is not happening—dreaming is. Leadership is happening when leaders and collaborators are *actively* seeking changes *now*.

"Change" means that leaders and collaborators seek to alter the status quo. While this may seem obvious, change is really substantive. Rost uses the term "real" to describe changes. To him, "*real* means that leaders and followers intend changes in people's lives, attitudes, behaviors, and basic assumptions, as well as in the groups, organizations, societies, and civilizations they are trying to lead."[41] He felt that change must be meaningful and "transforming." Thus, simplistic goals don't necessarily count as changes; *real* changes are those that have meaningful impact and transform our lives.

Envisioned Changes Reflect Mutual Purposes.

Leaders and collaborators must envision changes together and agree to seek them because they believe that those changes are beneficial for those in the influence relationship. According to Rost, changes "must reflect what the leaders and followers have come to understand from numerous interactions as the mutual purposes of the leaders and followers."[42] Rost purposely doesn't say that the changes must reflect the mutual purposes of *all* the leaders and followers. That, he realizes, would be too high a standard to be practicable. Nevertheless, to the extent possible, envisioned changes should represent the common direction and purposes of the leaders and collaborators.

This point is significant because it reminds us that leadership does not happen if the changes reflect only the leader's ideas. The leader must communicate the vision with the collaborators, and the collaborators must agree that the vision reflects their ideas for change. If not, the collaborators must be able to influence and work with the leader so that the vision reflects mutual purposes.

The word "purposes" is also important. Leaders and collaborators must envision mutual purposes, and those purposes are generally broader than goals. Purposes are the overarching reasons goals are typically pursued. For example, a goal in an organization may be to get 500 more customers by the end of the month, but its *purpose* would be to become a greater force in the market and position itself to be an industry leader. A goal in a volunteer organization might be to raise a certain amount of money by the end of the year, but its *purpose* is to serve the people it represents. Purposes, then, are more about mission than about goals.

So now you know what leadership is: the process of leaders and collaborators coming together through an influence relationship and seeking envisioned changes that reflect their mutual purposes. But how does that help you? You know what leadership is, but how do you *do* it?

E⁶: THE FRAMEWORK OF LEADERSHIP

You've come this far. You've learned the principles that underlie leadership, and you have a good working definition of leadership. You have now begun to understand leadership in more complex ways than most students ever do. Now it's time to learn how to put the understanding into practice.

Since a leader is *a person engaged in, and who intends to engage consistently in, a leadership process,* you need to *engage* in leadership. To help you do so, I've created a framework helps to bring leadership into reality.

The framework is called F⁶. It stands for the six activities that I am convinced make leadership come into fruition: envision, enlist, embody, empower, evaluate, and encourage. Certainly these are not the only words that could describe leadership, but it just so happens that taken together, they create a framework that is both memorable and representative of the definition

Envision
Enlist
Embody
Empower
Evaluate
Encourage

—THE LEADERSHIP FRAMEWORK

To see how this framework operates, let's look at an example. Let's say you want to lead your fellow volunteers to perform better so that your organization can reach its ambitious fund-raising goals.

To lead others to become stronger performers, you could

1. *Envision* ways in which they could better perform;
2. *Enlist* their support in shaping and pursuing exactly how to perform better;
3. Work to *embody* the principles and behavior you wish others to model;
4. Help them understand how to be better volunteers and *empower* them with the information, decision-making authority, and autonomy to do so;
5. *Evaluate* the vision, your ethics and performance, and their progress; and
6. Constantly and consistently *encourage* them to sustain the journey, to grow, and to become wiser, freer, more autonomous, healthier, and likelier to become servants themselves.

The same process could apply to starting a new student group or club, enhancing an organization in your community, strengthening the bonds of your family members, or raising money for a local charity.

E^6, in this light, is a framework for enacting leadership. Each activity in the framework is not necessarily chronological or mutually exclusive. With this in mind, you should not assess your leaders by what "stage" of E^6 they are in, or if they are faithfully following the framework. It is not my intention to give you *the* framework of leadership, just *a* framework that is memorable and representative of what I believe happens in leadership. Thus, this framework can serve as a guide for those wishing to navigate the waters of leadership, particularly for emerging student leaders.

The rest of this guide elaborates on this framework with ideas rooted in the principles and definition described above. Chapter two focuses on *envisioning*—how to create a personal vision and form a "rough draft" vision for you and your collaborators. Chapter three shows you how to *enlist* support of collaborators by refining your vision to meet mutual purposes, and how to communicate the final vision. Chapter four looks at leaders' *embodiment* of their messages. *Empowerment*, the subject of chapter five, outlines how to include participative processes in sharing authority, and how to create a conducive environment for your collaborators to become leaders themselves. Chapter six helps you understand how to *evaluate* the vision you are pursuing, your ethics and performance, and the progress of your collaborators. Finally, chapter seven provides examples to raise collaborators' self-esteem and self-efficacy through charismatic, compassionate, and supportive *encouragement.*

Each chapter is short and succinct, providing ideas that are user-friendly and context free, so that you can apply them to your own situation. At the end of each chapter you will find a list of Leadership Self-Check Questions, which will help you examine your purpose and progress.

The framework of E^6, like leadership itself, must ultimately lead to those you serve becoming stronger, wiser, empowered, and better cared for, and, most importantly, help them become leaders in their own right. This is no easy process, and these are high ideals to achieve.

Unfortunately, when someone describes higher ideals, particularly in leadership discussions, the naysayers come out of their corners. They cry, "It's too hard; it won't work; you can't expect people to be superheroes; people won't reach for such things." Their frenzied cries and pessimistic outpourings can overpower us, and often prevent us from trying. I ask, though, "What would happen if we all just *tried?*" What would society look like if we ducked the cynics' blows and pushed forward with full effort? What would society look like if we really did serve others and sought to transform one another?

Sure, it's relatively easy to assume that it takes a "super leader" to enact transformational, or servant, leadership. But we know differently. We've all had such leaders in our lives. It may have been our parents, a neighbor, teacher, friend, pastor, or colleague. They were just people, not superheroes. Their actions, though, could be described as heroic. Look at what they did for us. They guided us, inspired us, embraced us, and helped us reach for something more.

With all my heart I believe that you can do the same for others. Let's get started.

CHAPTER TWO

ENVISION

There is no more powerful engine driving an organization toward excellence and long-range success than an attractive, worthwhile, and achievable vision of the future, widely shared.

—BURT NANUS, *Visionary Leadership*

s the twenty-first century kicks into gear, we face a time of significant social, economic, and political change. The dilemmas and opportunities presented by these changes will need to be addressed by the next generation of leaders. Students are in a position of immense influence. Through a variety of academic and popular viewpoints and disciplines, we are able to study the issues that will dramatically affect our future. As we prepare to enter the "real world," we have the opportunity *and* the responsibility to assess the direction of our society and to begin envisioning its further positive development. We have to begin asking ourselves important questions about the direction of our families, communities, organizations, society, and global relationships.

Asking such questions is where leadership begins. "Where are we now?" and "Where could we go?" are the inquiries of great leaders and are the underlying components of their vision. Leadership is about a vision of the future and seeking to make that vision reality. Without a vision to guide us, we have no reason to come together and no direction once we are together. In other words, *you can't have goals, objectives, or strategies unless you first have a vision of what you want to achieve.* The vision is the reason we develop goals and plan strategies. The vision is the answer to the question "Leadership for what?" You lead to seek a vision.

So if, as a leader, you cry, "Let's go forward!" you'd better know where you are going. Having a vision gives people something to rally around, a dream to achieve, a reason to act, and a common purpose to pursue. A vision provides a sense of direction and a context for decision making, reflects organizational values and culture, recognizes and responds to a pressing need, and creates a strong future by providing direction for everyday actions toward its attainment.[43] In doing so, it creates meaning for everyone in the organization, provides a worthwhile challenge, energizes, brings the future into the present, and creates a common identity.[44] Thus, visions "accomplish multiple aims such as motivating and garnering commitment, aligning the organization, and building group identity."[45]

If leadership is rooted in service for a vision, then your first and most daunting task as a leader is to develop that vision. This chapter helps you begin this endeavor by discussing what a vision is, who develops it, and how you can take the first steps to creating one.

WHAT IS A VISION?

Many theorists have wrestled with how to define a vision. Here are some of their definitions:

- a set of idealized future goals established by the leader that represent a perspective shared by followers[46]
- cherished end values shared by leaders and followers[47]

- a mental model of an idealistic future or future perfect state, which sets standards of excellence and clarifies purpose and direction… inspirational possibilities that are value centered and realizable, with superior imagery and articulation[48]
- a realistic credible, attractive future for your organization[49]

As you can see, a common belief about visions is that they are about the future—where we are ultimately headed. It's the overarching description or explanation of what we are seeking. In reviewing the literature on developing visions, Gary Yukl, author of *Leadership in Organizations,* finds,

A vision should be simple and idealistic, a picture of a desirable future, not a complex plan with quantitative objectives and detailed action steps. The vision should appeal to the values, hopes, and ideals of organizational members and other stakeholders whose support is needed. The vision should emphasize distant ideological objectives rather than immediate tangible benefits. The vision should be challenging but realistic. To be meaningful and credible, it should not be wishful fantasy, but rather an attainable future grounded in the present reality. The vision should address basic assumptions about what is important for the organization, how it relates to the environment, and how people should be treated. The vision should be focused enough to guide decisions and actions, but general enough to allow initiative and creativity in the strategies for attaining it.[50]

This description is drawn primarily from organizational and business literature, and many leadership theorists remind us that leadership is not confined to organizations. When these theorists say "organizations," they mean traditional companies, firms, and bureaucracies. It's important to note, however, that you and your collaborators *are* an organization by definition. An organization can be defined as "two or more individuals who recognize that important goals can be more readily achieved through interdependent cooperative efforts than through individual action."[51] So when I say "your organization" throughout this guide, it can mean the organization created by you and your collaborators teaming up, or a more formalized organization like a company, firm, or bureaucracy you are working with or hoping to create.

Nevertheless, Yukl's description cited above gives a good overview of what a vision is and what it should do. You can see that a vision is not simply a goal, value statement, slogan, or strategic objective. Goals serve as stepping-stones to a vision. Value statements remind us what is important to us as we seek a vision (e.g., how people should be treated, standards of excellence). Slogans are short statements that remind us of a few values (e.g., "Quality is job number one.") as we seek a broader vision. And finally, strategic objectives are tangible results with deadlines that seek to bring us closer to the vision.

A vision is the ideal state you hope to achieve, the desirable future you hope one day to live in. To better understand what a vision is, it's helpful to look at a few examples.

Walt Disney

As Walt Disney developed his idea for the world's greatest play place, he realized he would need a vision that could inspire the commitment of investors, the media, and the American people. He described his vision this way:

> The idea of Disneyland is a simple one. It will be a place for people to find happiness and knowledge. It will be a place for parents and children to

spend pleasant times in one another's company: a place for teachers and pupils to discover greater ways of understanding and education. Here the older generation can recapture the nostalgia of days gone by, and the younger generation can savor the challenge of the future. Here will be the wonders of Nature and Man for all to see and understand. Disneyland will be based upon and dedicated to the ideals, the dreams and hard facts that have created America. And it will be uniquely equipped to dramatize these dreams and facts and send them forth as a source of courage and inspiration to the world.

Disneyland will be something of a fair, an exhibition, a playground, a community center, a museum of living facts, and a showplace of beauty and magic. It will be filled with the accomplishments, the joys and hopes of the world we live in. And it will remind us and show us how to make those wonders part of our own lives.[52]

Disney's inspiring and utopian vision was obviously well received, and many theorists have cited this example.[53] Though many theorists and consultants feel that vision statements should be briefer than this example, the quality of the themes represented is often more important than length. As Jon Katzenbach notes in *Real Change Leaders,* "Keeping it short helps make it memorable, but expressing a clear theme is more important."[54]

Disney's leadership brilliance stemmed from his ability to create a compelling vision. This vision served as an inspiring future for his collaborators, aligned organizational strategies to serve its tenets, and ultimately helped shape one of the most wondrous "dreams come true" of our past century.

The Automotive Company

An automotive company, whose mission is to make and sell cars, might have a vision like this:

> We will create an empowered organization to unleash our creativity and focus our energies in cooperative effort, and it will enable us to develop and build the best personal vehicles in the world, vehicles that people will treasure owning because they are fun to use, they are reliable, they keep people comfortable and safe, and they enable people to have freedom of movement in their environment without harming it.[55]

This vision is exceptional for several reasons. First, it is simple and idealistic—it doesn't confuse the reader with the myriad of action steps it would take to achieve this vision. Second, it arouses emotions that inspire enthusiasm and commitment. Third, it addresses organization members' desires to be empowered and serve others. Fourth, it is broad and flexible enough to allow organization members discretion in what steps to take to achieve it. Fifth, it sets a standard of excellence and stresses important values like comfort and safety. All in all, this vision statement is vivid, succinct, appropriate, and ambitious.

Texas Commerce Bank (TCB)

When TCB decided to massively redesign its banking processes, it needed a vision that would encapsulate why it was changing its organization. At first, TCB's leadership attempted to motivate collaborators by citing the $50 million savings and potential earnings. A few within the organization recognized this fallacy and instead created this simple vision: "Eliminate what annoys our bankers and our customers."[56] From this guiding vision, two important things happened. First, members of TCB deeply identified with the need to redesign to better serve its customers, and the vision was immediately accepted and championed. Second, it formed the guiding philosophies to all the change strategies implemented in the organization.

Though this vision statement seems simplistic, it served as an effective vision because it was incredibly meaningful to the employees of the bank. They were all aware of their customers' annoyances and recognized that significant changes were called for. This simple vision, which sounds very much like a slogan, gave them the guiding ideal they were seeking. They called it their vision rather than their slogan, because they knew it would never be completely accomplished—it was to be a vision perpetually chased but never fully realized. In the end, TCB's restructuring was immensely effective and returned more than the $50 million they had originally planned to make the heart of their vision statement.[57]

A Student Senate

The previous examples were given to show you how large businesses and organizations describe their visions. Student organizations and their leaders must also commit to developing vision statements. Again, the vision tells us the ideal state you hope to achieve—the underlying reason or purpose for coming together. What if a student organization began to form concrete visions that every member was committed to and strived daily to achieve? For example, suppose a student senate adopted the following vision:

> We will be a powerful force in the campus community avidly and loyally representing student interests and seeking to make those interests a reality. Through cooperative effort and collective action, we will obtain and distribute the resources students need to be successful in their college careers so that they can grow mentally, socially, physically, spiritually, and emotionally. We are servants to the students and will fight for them untiringly.

This vision, if properly communicated and shared among collaborators, could be an invaluable guiding force in the actions of the student senate. Of course, students can be very cynical and doubtful when a leader approaches them with a vision statement. We will address these concerns in the next two chapters. Nevertheless, we know that visions and vision statements are vital in order for successful leadership to occur.

It's important to note that the preceding examples were of vision *statements* and that visions do not always appear in such forms. For example, Martin Luther King Jr.'s "I Have a Dream" speech served as a vision for his leadership.

Mahatma Gandhi's everyday actions and teachings centered on a vision of pacifism and nonviolent symbolic statements. I chose the examples used above because they are concrete examples of how visions can be articulated. For students, I highly recommend formal vision statements for your organization so that it can be communicated succinctly and can create the kind of shared meaning that is the basis for mutual purposes.

Who Creates the Vision?

Many of us believe that leaders are like fortune-tellers; they can easily "see" the future and are blessed with some kind of gift. These amazing people single-handedly develop mutual purposes for themselves and their collaborators. Well, if you still feel this way, turn back to page one. Leaders don't develop mutual purposes in a vacuum. Remember, the definition of leadership includes the idea of leaders *and* collaborators seeking envisioned changes that reflect their mutual purposes.

At the same time, leaders often come up with preliminary visions. In a sense, they develop a "rough draft" of the vision. "The leader's search for opportunity"[58] helps them begin to visualize the future and form a personal vision. Peter Senge, author of *The Fifth Discipline,* argues that creating a personal vision *must* precede creating a shared vision.[59] You need an idea of what you want if you are going to create mutual purposes—you develop your purposes, then discern collaborators' purposes, then make them mutual. But you start with yours.

Thus, leaders' initial visions are often formed even before taking into account collaborators' needs and values.[60] This is because leaders often see shortcomings in the status quo and begin dreaming of a better future. After the leader conceptualizes a possible vision, he or she enlists collaborator input in order to develop mutual purposes. In this sense, leaders come up with a rough-draft vision and later enhance it with information from the collaborators to ensure that they are being served. This idea led Conger and Kanungo, authors of *Charismatic Leadership in Organizations,* to call leaders "principal assemblers of the vision."[61]

As a student leader, you will most likely be a "principal assembler of the vision." I say this because student leaders often start from scratch. They have to come up with a rough-draft vision, bounce it off others, reshape it, and then share it in hopes of gaining collaborator insight and participation in defining mutual purposes.

How do you begin to assemble the vision? I recommend keeping your eyes and ears open to what is happening around you. Bennis and Nanus, authors of *Leaders: The Strategies for Taking Charge,* noted that leaders seek input from others to define a vision and expend a

> substantial portion of their time interacting with advisors, consultants, other leaders, scholars, planners, and a wide variety of other people both inside and outside of their own organizations in this search. Successful leaders, we have found, are great askers, and they do pay attention.[62]

Leaders pound the pavement to come up with ideas. They talk to people. They ask what's missing. They do their homework and begin to see what people want. James Kouzes and Barry Posner, authors of the phenomenal book *The Leadership Challenge,* say,

> Leaders find the common thread that weaves together the fabric of human needs into a collective tapestry. They seek out the brewing consensus among those they would lead. In order to do this, they develop a deep understanding of the collective yearnings. They listen carefully for quiet whisperings in dark corners. They attend to the subtle cues. They sniff the air to get the scent. They watch

the faces. They get a sense of what people want, what they value, what they dream about.[63]

So you can see that you'll be instrumental in creating a vision, particularly a rough-draft vision. And doing so comes from spending ample time investigating what your potential collaborators want. The leader indeed does play a large role, maybe the largest, in shaping the vision.

No matter how good you are as "principal assembler" of the vision, it must, by the definition of "leadership," reflect mutual purposes in the end. As Bennis and Nanus eloquently remind us,

> In the end, the leader may be the one who articulates the vision and gives it legitimacy, who expresses the vision in captivating rhetoric that fires the imagination and emotions of followers, who—through the vision—empowers others to make decisions that get things done. But if the organization is to be successful, the image must grow out of the needs of the entire organization and must be "claimed" or "owned" by all the important actors.[64]

Your responsibility in developing the initial vision is paramount. Collaborators will look to you for some kind of vision. Indeed, "followers, who are often partners in an endeavor, look to leaders to interpret reality, explain the present, and paint a picture of the future."[65] The next section will help you begin a rough-draft vision that you will enhance later with collaborators' thoughts, needs, and dreams.

Developing a Vision

As Burt Nanus notes in *Visionary Leadership,* "Every leader develops vision in his or her own way, sometimes rationally and objectively, often intuitively and subjectively."[66] There is no magic formula for developing a vision of the future. This section poses questions for you to consider and explore in order to help you get the ball rolling. Of course, you won't be able to create a definitive vision just by reading this section. Indeed, according to Gary Yukl, "a successful vision is seldom created in a single moment of revelation, but instead it takes shape during a lengthy process of exploration, discussion, and refinement of ideas."[67] Once a vision begins to take shape, remember that visions are not static—they are dynamic and must constantly be assessed and developed over time. Hopefully, though, you will be able to generate a few ideas and begin the process of envisioning a better tomorrow.

Visioning is a combination of reality checking, dreaming, and brainstorming. And to do these things, leaders use the power of questions to assess the past, present, and future. They spend the majority of their time on two time frames: (1) questions about the present—"Where are we now?"—and (2) questions about the future—"Where could we go?" The following sections will help you assess the present and look to the future, and will remind you what your vision should ultimately do. You may want to do this alone at first and then involve more collaborators as you progress.

Assess the Present

Peter Senge, in *The Fifth Discipline,* reminds us, "An accurate picture of current reality is just as important as a compelling picture of a desired future."[68] Before you can paint a picture of tomorrow, you have to understand what today looks like. You have to study the current environment you are in. An active assessment of the environment is crucial to leaders' activities.[69] You have to look at the overall picture of the context in which you hope to lead. Is there an organization you wish to lead in? If so, according to Yukl,

To develop a compelling vision, it is essential to
have a good understanding of the organization
(its operations, products, services, markets, com-
petitors, and social-political environment), its
culture (shared beliefs and assumptions about the
world and the organization's place in it), and the
underlying needs and values of employees and
other stakeholders.[70]

Here are some questions to further consider if you wish
to lead in an existing organization and are seeking to assess
its present purpose and direction:

- What is the mission or purpose of
  your organization?
- What value does your organization serve?
- Who are the stakeholders inside and outside
  the organization?
- What is unique about your organization?
- What does your organization need to succeed?
- What values make up the organization?
- What are the strengths and weaknesses of
  your organization?
- What are the reasons your organization does
  what it does?
- Where is your organization heading currently?

- What is your organization the *best* at?
- Do the organization's members agree with where they are headed?
- How is the organization designed?
- Who are the organization's leaders?
- What is the culture like?
- What financial objectives drive the organization?

Spend some time considering these questions. You need a crystal-clear understanding about what your organization currently does, how it does it, and why it does it before you can begin to imagine what it should do in the future.

If an organization does not yet exist, and you are hoping to create one and lead it, you should still ponder the above questions and imagine what your answers would be. Also, you have to assess the current environment in which you live or work, to see whether there is a need for your potential organization. (Remember, I will use the word "organization" to mean either you and your collaborators as a team or a more formal entity like a company, firm, or bureaucracy.) Since leaders "actively search out shortcomings in the status quo,"[71] you may find that there is no current organization of people who do what you want to do. In this case, you are lucky in that you can begin to brainstorm about the potential organization's future.

Look to the Future

A Chinese proverb reminds us, "Change your direction, or you'll arrive where you're headed." If you've identified shortcomings in the status quo, this is where you begin to form ideas to respond to those problems. Maybe your organization is weak in several areas. Maybe there is no organization to do what you want to do. Whatever the case, your activities and thoughts need to become what Conger and Kanungo call "the leader's search for opportunity."[72]

Questions to help you look to the future could include

- What's missing now?
- What could be done better?
- What could we be the best in the world at?
- What do we really want to do here?
- Are there unexplored opportunities?
- What new ideas could benefit this organization?
- What haven't we tried to do?
- What do we really want to improve?
- Are there changes we will have to make soon?
- Whom are we not serving?
- What social, political, financial, technological, and environmental changes will we have to adjust to?

- What do we want to have accomplished in
  five years? Ten years? Twenty?

The Vision

When you begin to develop the vision, or put it into words, remember that it should reflect a strong theme and should emotionally engage people. In essence, the vision should serve two fundamental functions: provide the road map, and attach emotional appeal.[73]

To get you thinking further, themes and motivations for visions often reflect a sense of pride, a desire for greatness, a competitive spirit, service to others, doing the right things, and overcoming odds.[74] These themes often help create memorable, motivating, relevant, and effective visions.

Here are a few questions to further explore once you've developed a rough-draft vision:

- What must the vision end in or accomplish?
- Will everyone in your organization under-
  stand and support the vision?
- What values and ideals does it champion?
- How should the organization be best shaped
  to achieve the vision?
- Do you need to develop new policies?
- Do people need to be further trained?

- What incentives are there for collaborators to seek to attain the vision?

In addition, consider Burt Nanus's questions from *Visionary Leadership:*

- To what extent is it *future oriented*?
- To what extent is it *utopian*—that is, is it likely to lead to a better future?
- To what extent is it *appropriate* for the organization—that is, does it fit with the organization's history, culture, and values?
- To what extent does it set standards of excellence and *reflect high ideals*?
- To what extent does it *clarify purpose* and direction?
- To what extent is it likely to *inspire enthusiasm* and encourage commitment?
- To what extent does it *reflect the uniqueness* of the organization, its distinctive competence, and what it stands for?
- Is it *ambitious* enough?
- Is it *well articulated* and easily understood?[75]

These types of questions are crucial in developing an effective vision, so spend adequate time on each one.

What Next?

Assuming you've developed an idea of what your vision will be, you need to do two things. First, start thinking about strategies to attain your vision, and start drawing the "map" to the promised land. Though many leaders leave the more detailed planning to managers,[76] you will surely need to have some initial ideas about how to start moving forward. Once you start sharing your vision with others, they may love it and then ask, "How do we do this?" You need to have a few ideas to share with them. Consider these questions:

- What will you have to do?
- What will your collaborators have to do?
- What alliances will you have to make?
- What resources will you need?
- What technology will need to be used or created?

Second, you have to begin to think about (1) who you are going to share your vision with, and (2) how you are going to communicate it to them. In the next chapter I'll discuss in depth how to do this and, more importantly, how to enhance and finalize a vision that reflects mutual purposes.

This chapter has been about envisioning the future and sets the groundwork for what you will be doing throughout the leadership process. Make sure you've spent time considering the questions posed here, and that you have a good idea about what you want to do. Again, leadership is about seeking envisioned changes, and if you don't have an idea about what those changes are going to be, you are not leading.

Leadership Self-Check Questions

Ask yourself:

- Do I really understand the present context of the organization?

- Can I describe the exact mission of the organization?

- Can I describe the values that are most important in the organization?

- Whom does my organization serve?

- Whom are we not serving?

- Who are the stakeholders inside and outside the organization?

- What is unique about what we do?

- What do we need to succeed?

- What are we strongest at? Weakest?

- What are the reasons this organization does what it does?

- If we continue on this path, where will we end up?

- Does everyone agree with where we are headed?

- What's missing now?

- What could be done better?

- What do we really want to do here?

- What else could we be doing?

- What new ideas could benefit us?

- What can we be the best in the world at?

- What do we really want to improve?

- Are there changes we will have to make soon?

- What social, political, financial, technological, and environmental changes will we have to adjust to?

- What specifically will I have to do?

- What will I be asking collaborators to do?

- Will they be ready for the changes?

- What pushback will I receive with this vision?

- How will we begin to achieve this vision?

- Who will I bounce this initial vision off of?

- How will I communicate this vision to collaborators?

CHAPTER THREE

ENLIST

Good leaders articulate what people really need, but only when they understand what that need is. Then the power comes from the people, not because the leader tells them what to do, but because you are describing what they want and filling a void.

—SUSANA BARCIELA, *Insights on Leadership*

This is the chapter that will help answer the question "How do I go about getting collaborators?" In leadership literature, volumes have been written on how leaders "get" followers. Leaders can enlist collaborators by any combination of persuasion, charisma, power, creating a sense of urgency, or drawing an enticing picture of the future. What we know for sure is that "followers are more likely to select as their leader an individual who espouses their core values, beliefs, and aspirations."[77] This chapter will help you to (1) clarify your vision so that it reflects your and your collaborators' mutual purposes, and (2) communicate that vision.

All this discussion is aimed at helping you gain collaborators, because the timeless truth of leadership is this: if you enlist collaborators to help create a vision, then enlisting their support in taking action to move toward that vision happens automatically.

Though you may have an idea of what your vision is, remember, leadership is not about *your* vision. We have defined "leadership" as the process of leaders and collaborators coming together through an influence relationship and seeking envisioned changes that reflect their *mutual purposes.* Leadership, then, is about a vision coming from you *and* the collaborators. Their vision is just as important as yours. Leaders do not write on a blank slate. If the vision for tomorrow does not reflect collaborators' wants and dreams, then they will not join your quest to accomplish it.

This is an important point because, unlike management, leadership does not have a captive audience. Collaborators don't *have* to work with you. In management, because of hierarchical positions, people have to do what their managers want if they wish to keep their job. Leadership, on the other hand, must seek to influence others through the sheer attractiveness of the end goal. As Peter Block, author of *Stewardship*, reminds us, collaborators' enrollment in leadership is a *choice*. They can choose to follow and collaborate with you, or walk away. Their commitment and decision to join is based on their desire to pursue mutual purposes with you. They will only stay if they feel you are doing something worthy, something that reflects their desires. Thus, you need to make sure your vision is *their* vision, and articulate that to them effectively.

To help you do so, the following section will help you to make sure your vision is geared toward mutual purposes. In the final section of this chapter, I'll show you a way to communicate the "final draft" vision to potential collaborators to help further enlist their support.

RESHAPE YOUR VISION

As President Woodrow Wilson once said, "The ear of the leader must ring with the voices of the people." You need to spend tremendous amounts of time listening to the people around you and observing what they want. In the last chapter you should have come close to articulating the vision you want; now it's time to make sure it is one *they* desire as well.

If you want your vision to reflect mutual purposes, you have to (1) check your rough-draft vision against their values and desires by listening and asking questions, (2) relate the vision to collaborators who have a pulse on collaborator needs, and (3) reshape the vision to reflect mutual purposes.

Check Your Vision by Discovering Theirs

Is what I want what they want? This simple question will fundamentally affect leadership at every level. The problem with many would-be leaders is that they want others to follow them but have never asked this question. Too many assume what others want without doing their homework. If you believe in seeking mutual purposes, then you'd better start to find out some of your collaborators' purposes. If your desired collaborators don't want what you want, then they will not willingly and enthusiastically join you. The authors of *Charismatic Leadership* point out, "Followers are more likely to select as their leader an individual who espouses their core values, beliefs, and aspirations, *despite the fact that these may not always be clearly articulated by followers them-*

selves."[78] Thus, though your collaborators may not even have articulated their desires, your job is to get a grasp of them.

The only way a leader can do this is by a lot of focused, active listening and questioning. This sounds simple, and luckily for us, it is. This is the time to let your communication abilities shine. This is the time for you to get into meaningful conversations with your collaborators, to get their participation and input. To do so, I recommend that you (1) get to know people individually, (2) form small groups, and (3) check the vision against what you learned.

First, spend some time getting to know your collaborators *individually.* Here your role is that of *observer and interviewer.* Spend time with them one-on-one. Observe what they talk about when they discuss the future, and start noticing themes that keep coming up. Do people commonly talk about current problems or future possibilities? What seems to be bothering a lot of people? What are people suggesting needs to be done to improve their reality?

John Gardner, former secretary of health, education and welfare and advisor to six U.S. presidents, said, "A loyal constituency is won when the people, consciously or unconsciously, judge the leader to be capable of solving their problems and needs, when the leader is seen as symbolizing their norms..."[79] As a leader, you can not be judged capable if you are not first seen as someone who knows what your collaborators' problems and needs *are,* so start looking for common themes as an observer.

Then begin getting more specific information by taking on the role of interviewer. You don't have to do formal interviews, though that may work and you should consider it.[80] You can have conversations in which you try to get themes and answers to these types of questions:

- What do we value around here?
- What do you want to do in the future?
- What would you change around here if you could?
- What's missing?
- Where could we make a difference?
- What ideas do you have about making things better?
- What could we do together?
- Whom can we serve?

Second, form some *small groups* to discuss the future. Your role here will be that of *facilitator.* Ideally the groups should be relatively small: four to ten people. These gatherings should be fun, creative brainstorming sessions, in which you get people talking about what excites them and where they want to go. You are *not* trying to come up with a consensus on what to do. You are trying to come up with a bunch of ideas about what you *could* do. You don't have to be an expert facilitator to do this;[81] however, as a facilitator you should do these things:

- Encourage full participation and let everyone know that every contribution is worthwhile.[82]
- Focus on getting ideas out, not on criticizing or judging them.
- Give everyone ample and equal "airtime."
- Make the meeting fun, passionate, and forward-thinking.

Ask similar questions to the ones you asked people individually. All you're doing is trying to get themes and ideas that show people's values, hopes, dreams, and ideas about the present and the future. You won't be able to do this in one day. You'll have to spend some time here, but it will pay off. Take your time; pay attention; take notes.

Finally, after you've got the feel for what your potential collaborators are experiencing, what they value, hope for, dream of, and aspire to achieve, write down as many common themes as possible. Of course, not everyone will have precisely the same values and aspirations. Find the common core values and aspirations, the broadest, most pervasive themes. Here you want to begin comparing these themes to the themes of the vision. Your role here is as an *analyst*. You want to see if your rough draft vision in any way reflects what people are thinking of and want to achieve. Ask yourself, "Do these people want what I want?" and maybe more importantly, "Do I want what they want?"

Remember, leadership is rooted in service to collaborators. You are not in the leadership business to get solely what you want. You are here to serve others. So ask, "Now that I know what they seem to want, have I created, or could I create, a vision that would serve them?" If your rough-draft vision reflects the themes you've discovered, congratulations! If not, it may be time to ask if your vision really serves your collaborators at all. If it doesn't, it may be time to start the envisioning process over again.

"Shop" Your Vision

Supposing that you believe your vision to be something that reflects mutual purposes, it's time to "shop" it around to see if it is in line with collaborators' needs. This step is simple but crucial. You don't want to stand in front of the masses and scream, "I've got it!" until you're sure you've got it.

Try to get together a group of people—again, preferably a small group—who, you feel, understand or represent as many potential collaborators as possible. Sit down with them and simply begin with "I've got an idea." Articulate your vision as best you can, not as *the* vision but as an *idea*. Hold up your ideas and beliefs, not your arguments. The goal is to see what they think of the idea—that's it.

Ask what they think, and listen. Ask them questions like these:

- What do you think of this vision?
- Does it reflect what people around here want?
- Would people get excited about it?
- What would you change in it?
- Is there anything missing?
- Do you think it encompasses people's values and aspirations?

Let them punch holes in your vision. Let them support or argue against it. Let go of control and see where you end up. Release possession of your vision and let them shape it with theirs. They will either want to change it or keep the general idea the same. This is the litmus test for your vision. And this is the transformational point where *your* vision must become *their* vision, not because you've persuaded them but because they have helped create it.

Reshape the Vision

Finally, reshape the vision to reflect mutual purposes. This can be done at the same meeting or later on. After all you've done—created a vision, listened to others' desires, related your ideas to others—you should be able to answer this crucial question: *Does this vision for the future reflect mutual purposes?*

If it does, you're on your way. By creating a shared vision that reflects mutual purposes, you are creating a shared identity among your collaborators and you. And once people have a collective shared identity, they will avidly work together in pursuit of the shared goals.[83] People support and get excited about what they create. If they have a sense of ownership in the vision, they will have a sense of pride in moving toward its attainment. Work hard here. Too many would-be leaders power through this stage. When opposing views come up, they scramble to get it *resolved* instead of getting it *right*. Get the vision right. Get the right people involved. Take your time. Only then will you discover the high levels of excitement and passion that come from getting a group of people moving in a common direction.

COMMUNICATE THE VISON

The credible leader learns how to discover and communicate the shared values and visions that can form a common ground on which all can stand.

—JAMES KOUZES AND BARRY POSNER, *Credibility*

We know that collaborators join leaders in common endeavors for many reasons. Primarily, they do so because they are motivated to join a group when an attractive outcome is offered by the leader's vision.[84] You now have that vision. It reflects mutual purposes and offers attractive outcomes. Now you need to gain greater support for it by communicating it to a larger audience of collaborators. You may want to communicate the vision at a formal event (e.g., a meeting with all members of an organization, a press conference) or an informal one (e.g., a discussion group, a dinner meeting). Regardless of the venue, you will want to communicate the vision in person and convincingly.

Contemporary leaders face a difficult challenge. Society is generally cynical of leaders and their new visions and ideas. One can easily see the causes of this cynicism in political and corporate scandals over the years past and those that continue to plague us. Further, society is so overloaded with advertisements and mass communication that we filter out most messages. Leaders have the tough job of inspiring trust and attention amidst all the clutter.

Thus, you will also want to make sure you communicate the vision effectively. In *Charismatic Leadership,* Congo and Kanungo tell us that leaders effectively articulate their visions by discussing (1) the nature of the status quo and its shortcomings, (2) a future vision, (3) how the vision will remove the shortcomings, and (4) a plan for realizing the vision. Let's look at each of these steps individually.

The Status Quo and Its Shortcomings

In the last chapter I asked specific questions to help you assess the current environment or organization you are in. Now you need to take that information about the status quo and organize it into an effective, persuasive argument about why the status quo is insufficient. Presenting the status quo as unattractive, or even threatening, will create disenchantment and will lower resistance to the vision you will be advocating.[85] More importantly, it will make collaborators aware that what should be done is not being done. It will help them get a sense that things need to change, and your articulation of this need will begin to garner their support.

Leaders not only must articulate what is problematic

with the present, they must also create a sense of *urgency* that things need to change. For example, look at Martin Luther King Jr.'s masterful depiction of the present and the feeling of urgency for change he articulated in his famed "Letter from a Birmingham Jail":

> I guess it is easy for those who have never felt the stinging darts of segregation to say wait. But when you have seen vicious mobs lynch your mothers and fathers at will and drown your sisters and brothers at whim; when you have seen hate-filled policemen curse, kick, brutalize, and even kill your black brothers and sisters with impunity; when you see the vast majority of your twenty million Negro brothers smothering in an air-tight cage of poverty in the midst of an affluent society; when you suddenly find your tongue twisted and your speech stammering as you seek to explain to your six-year-old daughter why she can't go to the public amusement park that has just been advertised on television, and see tears welling up in her little eyes when she is told Funtown is closed to colored children, and see the depressing clouds of inferiority begin to form in

her little mental sky, and see her begin to distort her little personality by unconsciously developing a bitterness toward white people; when you have to concoct an answer for a five-year-old son asking in agonizing pathos: "Daddy, why do white people treat colored people so mean?"; when you take a cross-country drive and find it necessary to sleep night after night in the uncomfortable corners of your automobile because no motel will accept you…when you are forever fighting a degenerating sense of "nobodiness"—then you will understand why we find it difficult to wait.

Spend time articulating what state the present is in, and begin to make an urgent and reasonable call for change.

A Future Vision

This second step to articulating the vision, and why collaborators should enlist, is what leadership is about. This is the reason you've been working so hard to assess the present and dream of a better tomorrow. If the vision is attractive and exciting and reflects the hopes and dreams of your collaborators, they will likely join your cause.

You should passionately present the future as an ideal,

wonderful place. As Anita Roddick, founder of the Body Shop, says, "We communicate with passion—and passion persuades." You should use vivid ideas, language, symbols, metaphors, and stories. In describing the shortcomings of the status quo (step 1), President Ronald Reagan once called Washington, D.C., a "tarnished city." By the end of that particular speech, he presented a future vision (step 2) in which Washington would become "a shining city on a hill."

To use another powerful example from Martin Luther King Jr., let's look to his famous "I Have a Dream" speech, delivered on the steps at the Lincoln Memorial in Washington, D.C., on August 28, 1963. This speech is rightly referred to as the greatest oratorical performance in history, and you can see how he vividly depicted his future vision:

> I say to you today, my friends, that in spite of the difficulties and frustrations of the moment, I still have a dream. It is a dream deeply rooted in the American dream.

> I have a dream that one day this nation will rise up and live out the true meaning of its creed: "We hold these truths to be self-evident: that all men are created equal."

> I have a dream that one day on the red hills of

Georgia the sons of former slaves and the sons of former slave owners will be able to sit down together at a table of brotherhood.

I have a dream that one day even the state of Mississippi, a desert state, sweltering with the heat of injustice and oppression, will be transformed into an oasis of freedom and justice.

I have a dream that my four children will one day live in a nation where they will not be judged by the color of their skin but by the content of their character.

I have a dream today.

I have a dream that one day the state of Alabama, whose governor's lips are presently dripping with the words of interposition and nullification, will be transformed into a situation where little black boys and black girls will be able to join hands with little white boys and white girls and walk together as sisters and brothers.

I have a dream today...

This will be the day when all of God's children

will be able to sing with a new meaning, "My country, 'tis of thee, sweet land of liberty, of thee I sing. Land where my fathers died, land of the pilgrims' pride, from every mountainside, let freedom ring."

...When we let freedom ring, when we let it ring from every village and every hamlet, from every state and every city, we will be able to speed up that day when all of God's children, black men and white men, Jews and Gentiles, Protestants and Catholics, will be able to join hands and sing in the words of the old Negro spiritual, "Free at last! Free at last! Thank God Almighty, we are free at last!"

If you have not seen this speech, go and see it. If you have not read the speech, read it. This wondrous communication serves as the epitome of great leadership, and King serves as the epitome of a great leader.

As you shape your communication into an eloquent and persuasive message, remember to remind your audience that the vision is a mutual vision built on shared values, that it will benefit everyone involved, and that it may even benefit the greater society. Several organizational theorists have noted that shared values greatly increase personal and collective effectiveness,[86] so to help achieve these results, stress that the vision reflects shared values.

This is where your leadership shines: in the story you have of a better future, and your embodiment of that story. Speak with conviction and clarity and purpose, and you will find collaborators who will speak with you.

How the Vision Addresses the Status Quo's Shortcomings

This step involves showing how the vision will be better than the past. This is where you make some comparisons between the past and your future vision. You essentially talk about the "tarnished city" and the "shining city." This part of your communication sounds like this: "If we do this [vision], we will stop that [problem with status quo]." You are pointing out the problems with the status quo, and how the vision takes care of those problems.

Remind collaborators that creating the "shining city" will fix the problem and fulfill their hopes. Help them see that their best ideals about themselves, their self-concepts, will be reached. Leaders must tie the self-concepts of their collaborators to the missions they hope to engage.[87] Help them, then, to see that the vision takes care of the roadblocks that have been preventing them from being their best.

Returning to King's *Letter from Birmingham Jail,* we can see how his vision of gaining civil rights through nonviolent demonstration addresses the status quo's problems of being unable to negotiate with the segregated cities of the South.

> You may well ask: "Why direct action? Why sit-ins, marches and so forth? Isn't negotiation a better path?" You are quite right in calling for negotiation. Indeed, this is the very purpose of direct action. Nonviolent direct action seeks to create such a crisis and foster such a tension that a community which has constantly refused to negotiate is forced to confront the issue. It seeks so to dramatize the issue that it can no longer be ignored. My citing the creation of tension as part of the work of the nonviolent resister may sound rather shocking. But I must confess that I am not afraid of the word "tension." I have earnestly opposed violent tension, but there is a type of constructive, nonviolent tension which is necessary for growth. Just as Socrates felt that it was necessary to create a tension in the mind so that individuals could rise from the bondage of myths and half-truths to the unfettered realm of creative analysis and objective appraisal, we must see the need for nonviolent gadflies to create the kind of tension in society that will help men rise from the dark

depths of prejudice and racism to the majestic heights of understanding and brotherhood.

When you craft your message, you want to go to great lengths to show how the vision fixes the problems of the past and makes tomorrow even brighter.

A Plan of Action for Realizing the Vision

To make ideas effective, we must be able to fire them off. We must put them into action.

—VIRGINIA WOOLF

When people hear about promises of a better future, they are often skeptical unless they know there are clear and doable actions they can take to achieve the vision. You need to discuss some of the initial steps that you believe will be necessary to move toward the vision. Even if you don't know all the details of how to accomplish the envisioned changes, you can provide people with macro ideas about what needs to be done. For example, if a new student organization needs to be started, you don't have to know all the details for registering, getting funding, or what exactly the day-to-day operations of the new organization will be. You do need to tell people that they're going to have to figure out these things, that some footwork will need to be done to discover how to start a student organization. You also need to bring some people on board who can help you set the agenda and figure out steps to moving toward the vision. Simply put, leaders need to have some idea of what comes next and of what people will need to start doing to accomplish the vision.

In November 1993, then President Bill Clinton stood in the church where Martin Luther King Jr. had given his last sermon before his assassination. Clinton talked about an action plan. He gave a stirring speech to five thousand black ministers, one that earned him a place in *Lend Me Your Ears: Great Speeches in History.* He spoke about the country's responsibilities to teach nonviolence and address the disheartening status quo of "black-on-black" violence. Here are a few excerpts from the speech that talk about the status quo and a plan of action to address it:

> If Martin Luther King…were to reappear by my side today…what would he say?

> …He would say, I did not live and die to see thir- teen-year-old boys get automatic weapons and gun down nine-year-olds just for the kick of it…

> …He would say, I fought to stop white people

from being so filled with hate that they would wreak violence on black people. I did not fight for the right of black people to murder other black people with reckless abandon.

…Gunfire is the leading cause of death in young men…it is our moral duty to turn it around.

…We are trying to pass a bill to make our people safer, to put another ten thousand police officers on the street, to provide boot camp instead of prisons for our young people who can still be rescued, to provide more safety in our schools, to restrict the availability of these awful assault weapons, to pass the Brady Bill and at least require people to have their criminal background checked before they get a gun, and to say, if you're not old enough to vote and you're not old enough to go to war, you ought not to own a handgun.

…We need this crime bill now…We will, by God's grace, we will turn this around. We will give these children a future. We will take away their guns and give them books. We will take away their despair and we will give them hope.[88]

Clinton talked about some broad actions like providing safety in schools. He also talked about very specific actions, like putting 10,000 police officers on the street and passing the Brady Bill. Leaders must present some form of action, either broad or specific. They must show their collaborators a possible path to travel down. They must, with service in mind, help us get to "the shining hill."

These four steps to effectively communicating a vision are useful because, in effect, "the status quo is presented as intolerable, and the vision is presented in clear, specific terms as the most attractive and attainable alternative."[89] Collaborators will likely become disenfranchised by the status quo, inspired by the future, and encouraged to take the beginning steps towards the fulfillment of the vision. Howard Gardner, whom the *New York Book Review* called "one of America's most interesting psychologists," found that leaders are particularly skillful at developing and communicating stories about the past, present, and future. In his book *Leading Minds,* he noted, "They told stories—in so many words—about themselves and their groups, about where they were coming from and where they were headed, about what was to be feared, struggled against, and dreamed about."[90] These stories, which can be narratives, visions, dreams, embodiments, are what Gardner calls "stories of identity," which "constitute the single most powerful weapon in the leader's literary arsenal."[91]

In summary, if you've included mutual purposes in your vision and communicated it persuasively, collaborators will likely join you in a common endeavor. They will do so because they want what you want and vice versa. You've articulated all the shortcomings of the status quo and offered a compelling, progressive future. Now you can begin the collective actions needed to create that vision.

LEADERSHIP SELF-CHECK QUESTIONS

Ask yourself:

- Have I asked enough questions?

- Have I observed and listened to my collaborators' values and dreams?

- Do I understand what they want?

- How well do I know them?

- What would they change if they could?

- What do my collaborators expect from me?

- Have I found the strengths and shortcomings
  in the status quo and communicated them?

- Have I made a vision that reflects mutual purposes?

- Have I told them why the vision is attractive
  and what it will accomplish?

- Do I know what it will truly take to accomplish this vision?

- Do we all know the "game plan?"

Ask collaborators:

- Does the vision reflect ideals that you believe in?

- What can I do to better get "in touch" with the way people feel around here?

- Would you say that people believe I want what they want?

- Do people around here know why we're doing what we are doing?

- Would you say most people around here feel that we're doing something that is worth-while and inspiring?

CHAPTER FOUR

Embody

Let him who would move the world,
first move himself.

—Socrates

I n the last chapter, I stated that to enlist collaborators you need to know what they want, and articulate an attractive mutual vision. But that's not all there is to enlisting support. Of more importance is *how credible your collaborators perceive you to be.* You can have a great vision, adorned with all the bells and whistles of collaborators' values and needs. You can be a dynamic, persuasive communicator who articulates the vision with fervor and commitment. But in the end, if your collaborators do not believe you are credible—that is, they don't trust you and your capabilities—they will not join you.[92] This is why I've dedicated this entire chapter to the necessity of your embodying the ideals, values, expertise, and commitment needed to seek and attain a common vision. *If you don't stand for what you want others to seek, they will not stand for you.*

If you embody the ideals of your vision, not for show but because those ideals are a real part of you, collaborators perceive you to be trustworthy. They see that you "walk your talk" and "practice what you preach." They know you won't ask them to do what you don't do already. They know that you believe, practice, and live the ideals you are asking them to champion. They see you as a role model and a vivid image that reflects your message.

James Kouzes, coauthor of the best-selling books *The Leadership Challenge* and *Credibility,* reminds us, "People won't believe the message if they don't believe the messenger. People don't follow your technique. They follow you— your message and your embodiment of that message."[93]

Your messages, communicated verbally, and your embodiment of those messages, communicated by who you are and your actions, are the two main ways that you will influence your collaborators. Leaders communicate stories and must embody those stories through their traits and behaviors.[94] You have to talk, and you have to walk. If your stories and your traits and behaviors are inconsistent, you won't be credible. Consider Richard Nixon and, more recently, Bill Clinton. Both championed law and order—they both even had law degrees—and yet their actions violated those themes. Contrast these two with Martin Luther King Jr. and Mahatma Gandhi, who were willing to make personal sacrifices, such as going to jail—and, ultimately, even dying—for their causes. Their actions were consistent with what they championed in their stories.

Leaders who communicate stories and embody those stories build trust and loyalty[95] and ultimately become synonymous with those stories. When you think of Martin Luther King Jr., you think of the struggle for Civil Rights. When you think of Einstein, you think of the theory of relativity. When you think of Mother Teresa, you think of her caring for the poorest, most desperate people on earth. When you think of Lee Iaccoca, you think of innovation. When you think of Bill Gates, you think of the story of the computer age. When you think of Rudy Giuliani, you think of strength and compassion during crisis. These leaders not only championed their causes and beliefs through the stories and messages they related, they *became* the champions and embodiment of those causes and beliefs.

Such leaders are credible. They enlist support effectively because they communicate stories and visions, and they embody those stories and visions through their character and behavior. The last chapter helped you see how you can communicate your stories and visions. This chapter will help you consider how well you embody your message, and discusses ways you can more fully do so. Specifically, each section talks about (1) getting to know yourself, (2) gaining expertise, (3) being a role model, (4) the importance of passion, (5) the need for consistency, and (6) the importance of being a servant leader. The sections are short, but their themes are immensely powerful. These sections will help you become an example and a beacon of commitment, and thus help you gain the credibility you need to enlist collaborator support.

First, Know Yourself

Leaders seem to have an uncanny sense of what they stand for, believe in, and hope for. If you look at leaders in your life, it's easy to see that they have a sense of stability and strength of character. They know themselves and, often through their strong self-concept, inspire us.

Martin Luther King Jr. once said, "People are often led to causes and become committed to great ideas through persons who personify those ideas."[96] To repeat, people will ultimately join with *you* and collaborate with *you,* based on *your* ideas and personification of those ideas. In this sense, leadership is not a technique or a strategy of persuasion. As James Kouzes notes, "All the techniques and all the tools that fill the pages of all the management and leadership books are not substitutes for who and what you are."[97] So who are you? What do you stand for? What about you would make others join in your endeavors?

These are questions you need to ask yourself. You need to do a self-assessment and self-inventory of skills so that you can better know your strengths and purposes.

Exceptional leaders often take personal reflection time as they are leading.[98] You should do the same before leading.

Take some time asking yourself these kinds of questions:

- What are your three main beliefs about how people should be treated?
- Name four things you are an expert in.
- What are the three most pivotal moments in your entire lifetime?
- What did you learn from these moments?
- If you had only one year to live, what would you work toward?
- What would you like people to say about you after you die?

- How do you want to feel on a consistent basis?
- What are your top three values in your every-day life?
- What do you enjoy most about your life right now?
- What do you dislike the most?
- What activities are you passionate about?
- What causes would you fight for?
- What career would you be in if you could do anything?
- Ideally, what will you be doing in five years?
- What do you believe makes a good work environment?
- What makes a good home life?
- Name three lessons you would teach your children.
- Describe a time when you felt as though you had really accomplished something great.
- What were your two biggest failures, and what did you learn from them?
- What obstacles are preventing you from having what you want?
- Describe three people you greatly admire, and why.
- When things go crazy in your life, how do you best get centered again?
- What could you do in the next year to make the most meaningful improvement in your life?

- What do you do that people really appreciate?
- What contributions to the world do you make?
- What have you stood for in the past? What has been important to you in the past?
- If you had to, would you make personal sacrifices for your vision?
- Why are you starting to do this "leadership stuff?"[99]

These types of questions can help you begin the personal introspection needed to become a strong leader. Before you can embody ideals, you have to know what they are. So spend some time clarifying where you've been in life, where you are now, and where you hope to go. Doing so will help you gain the self-confidence that is nearly always noted as a trait of leaders.[100]

When assessing a leader's credibility, collaborators ask themselves questions about that person's trustworthiness, ability to inspire, and expertise.[101] While you are assessing your current state, ask yourself themes related to these inquiries:

- What makes me trustworthy?
- Have I developed a trusting relationship with my collaborators? How so?
- Do I have the ability to inspire others? How do I usually do it?

- What have I done lately to inspire and moti-
  vate others?
- What expertise do I have that collaborators
  know about?
- How will my collaborators measure me?
- Is my expertise relevant to collaborators' needs?
- What prior successes show my credibility?

You need to spend time assessing yourself and how your collaborators perceive you. This is an important task, maybe one of the most important and difficult that a leader must undertake. We know through examples from history that people who were self-confident, had a strongly developed self-concept, and had collaborators who perceived them as trustworthy, competent, and inspiring truly accomplished great feats. (Think Martin Luther King Jr., Winston Churchill, Lee Iaccoca, Pope John XXIII, Margaret Thatcher, and Mahatma Gandhi).

Gain Expertise

You don't always have to be an expert in a certain area to lead—but it helps. A leader's expertise or competence in the field he or she is working in is at the top of reasons why people decide to follow that leader.[102] High intelligence in general is almost always listed as a trait of leaders.[103]

I would venture to say that one of the biggest mistakes potential leaders make is to promise what they can't deliver. They claim that they have this knowledge, that skill, or some other exceptional ability. But over promising can lead only to one thing: failure. Remember, leadership is not a singular activity; it is a collective one. The know-it-all mentality that drives people to promise beyond their expertise is the same mentality that drives them to avoid including other people in decision-making—they think everything is about them, and they forget the power of collaboration.

To put it simply, if you don't have the knowledge, skills, or ability to make something happen, don't promise it. Be honest about your current level of ability. Don't be afraid to say, "I don't know how yet, but let's figure out how." Or "I don't know that yet, but I'll figure it out and get back to you." And once you say that, do all you can to get smart.

When Robert Kelley, author of *The Power of Follower-ship,* asked followers about their perceptions of their organizational leaders, he found something startling: two out of five bosses have questionable abilities to lead. A large majority of these questions arise from the perception that leaders do not have the appropriate knowledge to lead.

Here are the questions that arise from these findings:

- Will your collaborators believe you have the knowledge to lead?
- Do you feel that you have sufficient knowledge in your field?
- Have you done your homework on what is affecting your organization and your collaborators?
- Have you prepared yourself enough to lead?
- Are your skills sufficient?
- Do you know what you are talking about?
- What experiences have prepared you to lead in this context?

These types of questions are important for you to ponder, because your collaborators will be asking them of you. If you don't feel that you have enough expertise, do some homework. Go to workshops and seminars. Read trade magazines relevant to your field. Seek knowledge about your field any way you can.

BE A ROLE MODEL

> *Conviction is worthless unless it is*
> *converted into conduct.*
> —THOMAS CARLYLE

Leaders translate their values and visions into behavior and actions. They don't merely communicate the vision; they take steps every day to achieve it. They serve as vivid examples of the values and purposes they propose. Leaders serve as role models to their collaborators.

Unfortunately, only one in seven organizational leaders is someone whom collaborators see as a potential role model to emulate.[104] This statistic is frightening but believable. Look at your current work environment and judge your "leaders." Do they set examples? Do they walk their talk? Do they serve as someone you would want to emulate? When I ask this question around campus, I get just about the same statistic: one in seven.

Would you want your collaborators to say, "You know, our leader just isn't a role model for us"? Probably not. So you need to focus on setting an example. Collaborators need to see that you will go first; they need to see that it is possible; they need to see what they can and should do.

Along these lines, your being a role model helps people to (1) see that their leader is trustworthy and committed to the vision, (2) understand the beliefs, values, and behaviors that will help them realize the vision, and (3) become empowered by observing the leader's behavior and thus develop a sense of self-efficacy (a can-do, accountable, and optimistic attitude).[105]

When Gandhi stood before those who hated him, when Churchill created powerful speeches to verbalize defiance and courage, when Mother Teresa traveled the world to care for others, they set an example. When Martin Luther King Jr. went to jail without a struggle, in a symbolic and nonviolent message, he became a role model. As Howard Gardner, author of *Leading Minds,* notes, these types of leaders' "actions 'spoke' even more eloquently than their voices."[106] The examples they were setting helped their collaborators believe in them, helped them understand what they should do, and inspired them to do the same.

Many leaders break an important rule: to be a role model, you have to be seen acting for the cause. You have to be around to serve as an example and build credibility. The executives in the upper offices who are out of reach are those who become out of touch. These are the people whom collaborators say they will not emulate, because they've never seen anything *to* emulate. Leaders need to get down on the shop floor, work the cubicles, join their collaborators in the trenches. They need to show the way by example.

You need to seek constantly to be a role model. The essential question that all leaders must ask themselves if they want to embody the ideals they seek and to become credible is, *Am I setting the right example?*

BE PASSIONATE

Your dedication and passion to your vision will have a dramatic effect on your credibility. The collaborators you are seeking to serve need to see that you're committed to seeking the envisioned changes. "The followers begin to trust their leader when they perceive, beyond a shadow of a doubt, that their leader is unflinchingly dedicated to the vision and is willing to work toward it even if it means personal cost and sacrifice."[107] As an example, Lee Iacocca became a popular leader when he reduced his salary to just one dollar in his first year at Chrysler to show his commitment to his vision.

Burt Nanus, author of *Visionary Leadership*, noted, "Leaders live the vision by making all their actions and behaviors consistent with it and by creating a sense of urgency and passion for its attainment."[108] The best leader I ever had was someone who was consistent and had absolute and unwavering passion for our endeavors. She came to the office early and left last—not because she was a workaholic but because she *loved* what she was doing. She always immersed herself heart and soul in accomplishing our mission, which inspired a sense of urgency and motivation.

You need to share your enthusiasm and excitement for what you are doing with all your collaborators. Share your stories and experiences with them. Then you become a real person to them. They see your excitement, and in the words of the authors of *The Leadership Challenge,* you "sustain hope."

This simple premise, that you must be passionate about what you are doing, is immensely important. As the Bible says, "For if the trumpet gives an uncertain sound, who shall prepare himself for battle?" If you are uncertain or uninterested in your purpose, then why would collaborators join you?

Be Consistent

Collaborators look for consistency in their leaders' words and actions. If you believe with all your might for one day but doubt for six, if you say one thing and then do another, if you act nobly in the morning but selfishly in the afternoon, you are not consistent, you are not credible, and you are not a leader.

In the past decade we've seen immeasurable damage done to our confidence in our elected leaders' credibility because they were not consistent. When President Reagan claimed during the Iran-Contra investigation, "We did not trade weapons, or anything else, for hostages," and it later turned out that we had, he lost credibility. When President George Bush proclaimed, "Read my lips: no new taxes," and later raised taxes, his credibility was tarnished. When President Clinton promised, "I did not have sexual relations with that woman," and later said, "Indeed, I did have a relationship with Ms. Lewinski that was inappropriate," he lost credibility.

Leaders need to be truthful with their words and match their words with their actions. This is all part of walking the talk. Leaders who say one thing and then do or say another poison their credibility and commit one of the foulest violations of trust possible. Collaborators look to leaders, and join them, based on the leaders' promises. To break these promises, to abuse the position of leadership, is a disservice to your collaborators. Make sure you are being consistent. If you say it, mean it and *do* it.

Consistency is not only a measure of doing what you say you will; it is also a measure of your dedication to the vision. You are going to have ups and downs. Sometimes you'll find yourself full of doubt and despair, questioning your every move. Circumstances will not always rise to meet you. Things will go wrong. Your resolve to achieve your vision, and your consistent effort toward an envisioned purpose, will greatly contribute to your credibility.

BE A SERVANT LEADER

Leaders need to embody what their collaborators feel that a leader should be.[109] Nearly every definition of a leader comes down to a person who "guides" or "inspires" or "serves." All these terms fit the description of servant leadership.

Your collaborators have to know that you are embodying ideals that will benefit them, that you are serving them. As Kouzes and Posner note in *Credibility*, "The people's choice [for a leader] is based not on authority, but upon the leader's perceived capacity to serve a need."[110] Are you serving your collaborators' needs? Are you helping them to grow, to become wiser, healthier, freer, and more autonomous, and to achieve higher levels of motivation and morality?

Ultimately, you are a servant. You are here to serve the needs and desires of your collaborators and help them become greater. This is the essential theme of this book, and the most important idea in this section. For in the end, your collaborators must sense that you are here for them. All the ideas in this guide mean nothing if they are being used solely for your advancement.

It's easy to assume, after I've said that you have to know yourself, be an expert, be a role model, be passionate, and be consistent, that to be a leader you have to be some kind of hero. But that's not how it is. As Robert Kelley, author of *The Power of Followership,* reminds us, "Be less of a hero and more of a hero maker." The best leaders give other people the stage and seek to help them become better at what they do. They take care of them and build their competence and confidence. They *serve* their people.

LEADERSHIP SELF-CHECK QUESTIONS

Ask yourself:

- What are my convictions about the way people should be treated and the way work should be done?

- Is my conduct in line with those convictions?

- Do people around here trust me?

- What can I do to become an expert in this area?

- Will my collaborators believe I have the ability to lead?

- What prior success shows my credibility?

- Have I done my homework and gotten the information I need to lead?

- Are my words and actions consistent?

- Do I act like a role model for my collaborators? How?

- Do I really care for what I'm doing right now?

- Have I been serving the best interests of my collaborators?

Ask collaborators:
- Do my words and actions seem consistent?

- Would you say people around here trust me?

- What can I do to be a better role model?

- What do you think about the way I treat people?

- Would you that say people think I work hard for what I want them to work hard for?

- What else could I do around here to help serve others?

CHAPTER FIVE

EMPOWER

When [a good leader's] work is done,
His aim fulfilled,
They will say,
"We did it ourselves."

—LAO-TZE, *Tao Te Ching*

Empowering collaborators is a duty of servant leaders. Remember Greenleaf's test of a servant leader? He asks: Do collaborators grow as persons? Do they become healthier, wiser, freer, and more autonomous? The way to make these things happen is through empowerment. Remember, leadership is not management.

Leadership is *empowerment,* whereas management is *control.* If as leaders we seek to control our collaborators' every decision and action, they don't become more autonomous or wiser. They don't become freer. They simply do not grow. If someone ties your shoelaces for you every day of your life, you'll become dependent and you won't learn. Empowering leaders let go of the need to control, encourage people to define their realities and future visions, and ask them to participate actively in common endeavors that they have helped to define. When leaders give up control, collaborators take responsibility and continually become wiser and more autonomous through their experiences.

Though they may not have used the word "empowerment," nearly all leadership theorists, past and present, talk about its ideals. Allowing people the right to make decisions and take actions that affect their lives and organizations is at the center of many leadership philosophies. Indeed, empowerment is a *right* of collaborators, not something to be thrust upon them. Some collaborators may simply not want to participate in some decision making.[111] Others may want to be heavily involved.[112] Regardless, collaborators, as mutual architects of the purposes in leadership, need to be given choices in how involved they will be in decision making, and in what actions they take to achieve those purposes.

These ideas led to the empowerment approaches of the past two decades in management and organizational theories. Empowerment has become the big buzzword and is typically referred to as "efforts to enhance employee commitment and productivity through encouraging participation and involvement in organizational settings."[113] Quality circles, total quality management, work teams, and self-directed work teams are all examples of efforts to allow the employees of organizations to learn and grow through participation in their work. As noted in *Leading Organizations*, "The concept is straightforward: Organizations push down decision-making responsibility to those close to internal and external customers, and employees take charge of their own jobs."[114]

The move to empowerment was an obvious one. Some people, particularly the disempowered employees, wanted more of a say in what was happening around them, how they were working, and for what purposes. Freeman and Rogers, authors of *What Workers Want*, found,

> American workers want more of a say/influence/representation/participation/voice (call it what you will) at the workplace than they now have. Workers want greater say both because they

think it will directly improve the quality of their working lives and because they think it will make their firm more productive and successful (which also enhances their work lives over the long run). Employees want greater workplace participation as individuals and as part of a group as well.[115]

Reg Theriault, a social critic and author of *How to Tell When You're Tired,* puts it plainly when he says that some workers just want management to "get the hell out of the way."[116] Of course, employees can't have all the say at work, and management can't simply disappear. But as George Cheney, author of *Values At Work,* notes,

> Though we may decide it's unrealistic in a particular case for all employees to have a shaping influence on corporate or organizational policy, we can say more confidently that everyone ought to have some capacity to affect the conditions and requirements of work.[117]

The idea of empowerment seemed natural as workers and management finally began to realize something the authors of *The Human Touch* found: "Executives and managers are *not* responsible for knowing the solutions to all the company's problems. That's what the experts are for – and the experts are always the people who actually do the job for you on a daily basis."[118] Management may have realized that employees have significant input and need to contribute to decisions, and this realization has led to a proliferation of empowerment programs in the workplace in the past two decades. And these programs pay off. Employees who work in jobs that provide high levels of autonomy and information sharing (two foundational elements of empowerment) have higher levels of performance than other employees[119] and report higher levels of satisfaction with their work.[120]

The authors of *High-Involvement Leadership: Changing Roles for Changing Times* found several additional benefits to empowerment. First, leaders who are empowering are more committed to the organization, have greater job satisfaction, and have less role ambiguity and role overload. Second, organizations become stronger as empowerment improves upward communication, helps create speedier responses to requests and problems, and improves coordination across the organization. There is significant improvement in customer focus and the quality of products. Finally, empowered members of organizations are more motivated, believe they are more effective on the job, and report improvements in the quality of life at work.[121]

"Empowerment" has a slightly different meaning in leadership contexts than in management or organizational theory. In leadership, it is a right and responsibility of the members to make decisions together so they can seek mutual purposes. In management, "empowerment" typically refers to a way that organizations can produce more and "get more out of" employees.

In leadership, empowerment is not used to "get more out of people" or increase efficiency. Rather, it is simply a *responsibility* that a leader has to allow collaborators to make decisions and take actions that affect their lives and their organization. Empowering collaborators allows them to be freer, more autonomous, and ultimately wiser as they learn through their experiences. It helps them achieve "higher senses of motivation" by letting them seek purposes that they helped define.

As Robert Kelly notes in *The Power of Followership*, exemplary followers are not uncritical and passively engaged in their environments. They want to be part of the process. They are independent, critical thinkers who are actively engaged in leadership. They want to make decisions and be involved because they are partners in the endeavor. Leadership, by definition, gives them "ownership" of mutual purposes, and they want to be able to affect the choices of how to reach those purposes.

As mentioned, your job as a servant leader is to empower others. Indeed, collaborators' reports of the level of empowerment they feel are directly and significantly tied to how their leaders make them feel.[122] Empowerment is not an overnight accomplishment. It is a day-to-day, progressive activity that requires fundamental changes in attitudes toward participation and control. You have to realize that your collaborators should—and have the right to—participate in decisions. You have to realize that to empower, you have to give power. The ideas that follow can't be served to your collaborators in one day— they must be integrated slowly, steadily, and supportively.

To feel empowered, collaborators must feel that they (1) have the proper knowledge, skills, and ability to make decisions; (2) have the freedom and authority to do so;[123] (3) are supported by, and trust, their leaders; and (4) will be rewarded and recognized for taking action. Of course, the perception and behaviors associated with empowerment ultimately reside in the individual,[124] but leaders have tremendous influence in shaping those perceptions and behaviors.[125]

To help you in the process of empowering your collaborators, this chapter is broken up into four sections. Section one discusses education and training, section two looks at establishing participation, section three looks at shaping a supportive environment, and section four explores rewarding and recognizing collaborators' efforts.

INFORM AND EDUCATE

In empowering collaborators, above all you must remember "the vital teaching role of leadership."[126] Leaders often have to teach collaborators about people, concepts, ideals, values, skills, and environments that may affect them. Certainly, the leader is not some all-knowing presence, but leaders often do have information that is absolutely critical to collaborators. Thus, as Gardner says, "Leaders teach the vision, its values and goals and specific techniques to operationalize the vision, values and results...so collaborators can lead themselves."[127] Along with teaching about the vision, leadership is also about fostering learning, offering choices, and building consensus.[128]

A person's motivation to perform a task is directly linked to that person's belief that she has the ability to perform the task.[129] If one of your collaborators doesn't believe that he can do something, of course he will have little motivation to try. Since you are trying to help collaborators achieve higher levels of motivation, you first need to make sure they have the information they need to do something.

Keep Collaborators Informed

People need to be constantly updated on what's happening. They need to be sufficiently alerted and educated on changes, concerns, and contexts that affect their lives. They need to know the rationale for the things they are doing. Keeping them informed means getting them necessary access to organizational documents and people in the organization, no matter how "high up the ladder." If groups are going to make good decisions and take responsible actions, they need good information.[130]

Create Educational Opportunities

One of the main reasons organizations fail is because people don't have the knowledge or skills needed to do their jobs.[131] In every way possible, allow your members to further their education through programs, classes, seminars, and experiences.

Organizations spend over $1 billion on training each year. When people are asked why they join particular organizations, they often say that it's because of the training they will receive. Training is important. Whether formal or informal, individual, group oriented, or computer based, training allows people to broaden their knowledge and apply new concepts to their work efforts.

Education focusing on participation, negotiation, and collaboration is particularly relevant to empowerment ideals. As Stanley Deetz, author of *Transforming Communication, Transforming Business,* notes, "People are not born with the skills for effectively making decisions. Democratic skills, like any quality of civilization, must be learned."[132]

Encourage Risk, Experimentation, Creativity

People don't learn if they don't try, and they don't try if they're scared of failing or being reprimanded. Let your collaborators know that experimentation and creativity are championed, that mistakes are fine as long as one learns from them.

The level to which collaborators will begin to be empowered through education can be measured by the degree to which they agree with these statements:

- "I feel competent to perform the tasks required for my position."
- "I feel adequately prepared to perform my job."
- "I have the skill to excel in my job."[133]

CHAMPION PARTICIPATION

Since leadership is about mutual purposes, individuals who choose those purposes should have the ability to make decisions about how to attain them. We know from organizational literature that if people believe they have little control in their work environments, they become stressed.[134] This stress reduces motivation and ultimately affects whether the person wants to be involved in the organization. Knowing this, it is vital that you allow participation in your organization. Again, a leader has to recognize collaborators' *right to make decisions and take actions that affect their lives and their organization.*

This guide does not seek to propose what structure your organization should take. Much has been written about the "flat" organization, the "centerless" organization, and the "upside-down" organization. There are certainly a variety of structures for promoting and enacting participation and workplace democracy programs.[135] Job enrichment programs, quality circles, workplace quality-of-life programs, and self-directed work teams are implemented to encourage and support employee involvement and participation.[136] I believe that the idea of a flatter organization is generally a sound one, whose benefits were readily apparent in the 1990s. Nevertheless, different purposes call for different structures. The U.S. Army needs a precisely defined hierarchical organization; team-based organizations often do not.

Regardless of the organizational design and structure you choose, be very conscious of how much influence you are giving your collaborators. The "depth" of control that members have can ranges from "No right to any say; or right to make suggestions only" to "Workers have a majority of votes (or more) in the decision-making (workers decide)."[137] How much say will your collaborators have in making decisions?

Remember that your job is to serve them and accomplish purposes that you both have defined as important. This means that you need their continued input and support, and if you choke out their influence, you lose.

Certainly, participation by many members of an organization can create challenges. Decision making may take longer and may be more difficult simply because members have different backgrounds and knowledge.[138]

Nevertheless, if you really believe in mutual purposes, you not only must champion participation but must promote democracy. As George Cheney and fellow organizational communication experts note, "Democracy extends simple participation in the workplace by ensuring that the individual has a voice, may express an opinion that means something, and has the potential for 'making a difference' in the larger organizational context."[139] If possible, I believe we should approach a more ideal communication structure by creating democratic organizations in which

> Every member should adopt the *perspective of an owner*, information should be readily accessible, structures should be shaped by those at the bottom of the organization, and interactive discussions and negotiations of values and ends should occur on a regular basis.[140]

Of course, the number of your collaborators—and, as a result, your organization—may become so large that "true" democracy, in which everyone has a voice, becomes difficult.[141] Nevertheless, leadership, by definition, seeks changes that reflect mutual purposes, and you owe it to your collaborators to ensure they have a voice that can "make a difference" in what happens to them. As we saw in chapter two, you should seek to include as many collaborators, or representatives of those collaborators, as possible in creating a vision. Collaborators also need to be included in, and participate in, decision-making processes. Before asking others to make decisions or participate, though, you need to take into account how much information and education collaborators have, your relationship with them, their ability to perform a given task, and their degree of motivation to perform it.[142]

In the end, if collaborators are not involved in some significant level of decision making and participation, we forgo the idea of mutual purposes, forget who we are serving, and forget who the real experts are.

Empowerment means giving people a say, giving them a voice. It also means giving them authority and discretion to do what they believe needs to be done. Empowerment means that collaborators don't ever have to say, "I know it's a dumb policy, but there's nothing I can do. It's my job, and I have to follow the policy. Sorry, I wish I could help you."

One promising way that organizations are enacting such ideas of empowerment is by creating self-managed, or self-directed, work teams. Self-managing teams are peer groups (ten to fifteen people) that make all the decisions, do all the coordination, and perform all the work required to build the products or perform the tasks under their responsibility.[143] The team supervises itself; there is no first-line supervisor. The team hires, fires, and coaches its members; coordinates directly with other departments; and sets its own work schedule. The team has extended autonomy and is basically guided by the organization's vision.

Some possible benefits of such teams include increased employee motivation, productivity, commitment, and identification with the group, and more participation, with members playing a larger role in the organization's day-to-day operations.[144]

Negative consequences of self-managed work teams include added time and energy commitments from members, the need for members to identify strongly with the goals of the organization, and pressure on members to learn how to collaborate effectively.[145] To move away from these negative consequences, teams need to make sure that all voices are heard and respected and that a safe environment is created and maintained in which members are able to constantly refine and improve their conditions.

Whether you include teams in your organization is not the point here. The point is that team ideals such as democracy and participation can help you achieve mutual, collective purposes through mutual, collective action. Many organizations question whether democratic ideals can work in their environments, but as Deetz notes, "The bottom line is: Meaningful democratic participation creates better citizens and better social choices, and provides important economic benefits."[146] These are the results of great leadership.

And great leadership doesn't produce dictators or autocratic leaders. Great leadership, through championing participation and its democratic roots, produces leaders who are facilitators, stewards, servants, coaches, and teachers.[147] These leaders allow other people to have authority and control, and a less hierarchical organization is built. Successful organizations of the future will eliminate traditional hierarchical systems and move to work teams or other participatory systems.[148] And successful leaders of the future will move to more participative relationships with collaborators.

Empowerment is about giving people the authority to make decisions that affect their lives. Each member of your organization should take the perspective of an owner since they've helped shape the purposes you are pursuing. Is this simple? No. Is it worthwhile and empowering for everyone involved? Absolutely.

The level to which collaborators feel that participation is championed can be measured by how much they agree with these statements:

- "I am consistently asked for my opinion in important matters."
- "I have the authority to make decisions that need to be made."
- "[Leadership] trusts me to make the appropriate decision."[149]

HELP SHAPE THE ENVIRONMENT

Organizations with a positive environment or culture have members who feel empowered.[150] Shaping a positive environment is critical for leaders because "empowerment may be more of an organizational issue than a personal/interpersonal issue."[151]

Much of the popular management literature of the 1990s made it sound as if leaders could simply shape the environment and culture of an organization by sheer will and in a limited time. Many managers were led to implement a barrage of short-term programs to define and "fix" the culture of their organizations. Most of these programs failed because culture is not a ready-mix recipe. Just as in larger human societies, the culture of organizations has deep roots in roles, relationships, myths, routines, understandings, and assumptions. These roots cannot be dug up and replanted easily. Culture is developed and evolves over much time and through the reciprocal influence of communication by everyone in the culture—it is influenced not just by what the leaders decide are the "right" inputs.[152]

Yet leaders make a significant difference. I've been a member of many organizations that had the potential to be empowering, but where a sole leader stifled and choked any conception of empowerment. Peter Senge, in *The Fifth Discipline: The Art and Practice of a Learning Organization*, notes that leaders bear "an almost sacred duty" of creating conditions that allow people to grow and have productive lives. Leaders can begin to help shape these conditions by (1) stressing a community metaphor, (2) building a high-trust culture, and (3) promoting open communication at all levels of the organization.

Build Community

Jim Autry, author of *Love and Profit,* shows us what community at work is all about:

> By invoking the metaphor of community, we imply that we in business are bound by a fellowship of endeavor in which we commit to mutual goals, in which we contribute to the best of our abilities, in which each contribution is recognized and credited, in which there is a forum for all voices to be heard, in which our success contributes to the success of the common enterprise and to the success of others, in which we can disagree and hold differing viewpoints without withdrawing from the community, in which we are free to express how we feel as well as what we think, in which our value to society is directly related to the quality of our commitment and effort, and in which we take care of each other.[153]

This is as eloquent a description of a community as any I have heard. It is a description that values mutual purposes, openness, contribution, commitment, and compassion. It is a description that you want your collaborators to use when describing your organization.

John Gardner reminds us, "Skill in the building and rebuilding of community…is one of the highest and most essential skills a leader can command."[154] You need to invoke this community metaphor as much as possible, and not just for show, but to really *create* this type of environment. Poor would-be leaders throw around these types of metaphors to cover up inequalities and abuses. They say, "We are a family, a community," and at the same time practice behaviors and implement programs that say, "You are not important; we are in the business of making money, and that's all that matters." Great leaders, on the other hand, champion and practice these types of metaphors in order to create an environment that can design mutual purposes and collective, participative action. Great communities feel as though the work being done is deeply meaningful, challenging, and supported.

Your collaborators need to know they are heard, trusted, supported, and cared for. They need to hear that they are fellows in an endeavor, that one person's gain or loss is everyone's, that together, standing side-by-side, they are stronger than they could ever be alone. As a group bound together in a common interest, people believe that they can tackle the realities of the world and push back the frontiers of tomorrow. As one prominent psychologist notes, "The stronger the beliefs people hold about their collective capabilities, the more they achieve."[155] Your job is to help people build these beliefs by stressing that they are a capable community united in mutual purpose, and that through collective will and action they can achieve that purpose.

Build a High-Trust Culture

In a climate of trust, individuals can give open, candid reactions to what they see as right or wrong. In trust cultures there is little manipulation, few hidden agendas, no unreasonable controls, no saccharine sweetness that discounts real problems.

—G.W. Fairholm, *Perspectives on Leadership*

Not only is being trustworthy the key to your credibility as a leader,[156] it is also the key to the success of your organization. If people don't trust one another, they don't work together in a way that achieves the best results. They withhold information and feedback and question one another's intentions. In their effort to protect themselves, they cast a wary eye on the other members and the organization as a whole.

The authors of *The 100 Best Companies to Work for in America* say that a great place to work is one where you trust the people you work for, have pride in what you do, and enjoy the people you work with.[157] Looking at this list, it's easy to see how the second and third ideas can't happen without the first. You probably won't have much pride in your job if you're always fearful or mistrustful of your coworkers, and you won't enjoy your coworkers if you are constantly questioning their intentions and wondering what they're up to behind your back.

To create an environment of trust, leaders have to give collaborators trust and allow them to experiment and fail without fear of punishment.[158] Collaborators need to know that even if they really mess up, they are still accepted as individuals. Leaders need to create real relationships with their collaborators and listen to their concerns and ideas. In this sense, successful leadership will be measured by "the degree to which the leader's behavior towards group members is characterized by mutual trust, development of good relations, sensitivities to the feelings of group members, and openness to their suggestions."[159]

According to the Drucker Foundation, when people feel that there is trust in organizations, "they're encouraged to look horizontally across the organization for influences and collaboration, rather than upward to their bosses."[160] *Synergy happens at all levels of the organization as members believe that they can be creative and responsible without being dismissed or ridiculed.*

Trusting environments will be the result of a new paradigm of leadership rooted in service. As the service-rooted book *Insights on Leadership* notes, "Making it safe for teammates to be honest and being accountable to change, grow, communicate, and resolve differences in a spirit of mutual respect is the foundation of this new paradigm."[161] Creating a trusting environment can begin only with you. You have to embody trust. If you want your members to trust one another, you first have to trust them. If you want trust to grow throughout your organization, you have to be honest, candid, caring, supportive, open, collaborative, and accountable.

Promote Open Communication

Communication is *the* vehicle through which leadership happens.[162] Leaders spend 80 percent of their time communicating with others.[163] Maintaining a "full, open, and decentralized communication system" is absolutely imperative to empowered organizations.[164] The way to promote open communication is to stress the two ideas we've just discussed: the creation of a community environment and a high-trust culture. I say this because we know that the perceptions people have about emotional support, trust, and friendship dramatically affect their communication with others.[165] If people don't feel that their environment supports them, if they don't feel that they can trust the people in that environment, they aren't likely to communicate openly in that environment.

It is through communication that a community is built and trust garnered. So you need to promote open communication in every way that you can. The more candid, collaborative, and compassionate you can be, the more you help create effective two-way communication. The more you listen, the more your collaborators will understand their roles, believe you are trustworthy, be satisfied, and be part of effective groups.[166]

Ask people to talk to one another about different ideas. Form discussion groups. Make the rounds in the organization, talking about more than just work. You want multiplexity in communication—to speak with others about a variety of topics. People with multiplex relationships might share "information about work, personal issues, and innovative ideas."[167] They tend to communicate more frequently and have a more "intense, supportive, intimate, and influential" relationship than people who discuss only work.[168]

Further, these relationships tend to reduce uncertainty and spur innovation. The more that people feel free to discuss ideas openly, the more the organization will thrive.

The members must also be comfortable enough to gripe, complain, or raise concerns. This can't happen if power and fear stifle discussion. We know that there is a great reluctance for subordinates to communicate negative information to their superiors.[169] But in open communication environments, built by community and trust, they are willing to gripe because they know they will be heard and responded to. In *The Human Touch,* Arnold and Plas remind us that gripes "need to be tracked down and brought into the open rather than stifled, contained, or ignored,"[170] and that when a gripe is discovered, "you've located that aspect of the job or the corporation that an individual has energy and commitment for improving."[171] If you don't listen to people's gripes and concerns, they will become disenfranchised, feel they don't count, and decrease their commitment to your organization.

The ideals of community, trust, and open communication can and will dramatically influence your organization. They can inspire people to come together in common endeavors, take collective action, and positively steer themselves in useful directions.

Recognize and Reward Participation

Members who are empowered want to feel recognized and rewarded for their involvement, and when they are not, they become discouraged.[172] On the other hand, people report higher satisfaction when their leaders provide them with recognition, rewards, and positive feedback.[173] Has a leader ever not recognized your contribution? When I ask students that, they seldom have to think long to recall their negative feelings about a time when they were not appreciated. No doubt you, too, have been part of a project where you were not recognized for your contributions. When this happens it hurts, you feel cheated, you question other people's involvement, and you are less likely to give your full effort next time.

When you empower others, you are asking them to take on increased responsibilities. And as psychologist Albert Bandura of Stanford University points out, "People are not too eager to shoulder the burdens of responsibility."[174] So if you've given them a choice (which you should), and they shoulder the responsibility and seek to make decisions that affect themselves, you should recognize them. If they feel that they are "going out on a limb" and are frightened of potential repercussions rather than inspired by recognition, their performance will be hampered. A simple "I appreciate your involvement and contribution" goes a long way. In their best-selling book *In Search of Excellence,* Tom Peters and Robert Waterman found that excellent leaders exert a tremendous amount of effort to provide positive reinforcement for those who have taken action that was valuable to the organization.

Organizational rewards, monetary or otherwise, should also be set up to recognize those who put full effort into improving their environment. As student leaders, we often do not have the resources to give financial rewards for participation and performance. However, we have vast resources of creativity and collaboration that we can use to recognize people. I've been part of student teams where we gave out cards, photographs, certificates, mugs, T-shirts, and thank-you cards. We thanked people publicly in front of the groups they worked with. We got their names in the paper and on the radio. We did everything we could to let those individuals know that they were recognized for their efforts. These types of small gifts during and after challenging projects help beyond words. They show appreciation. They show gratitude. They show acceptance. They show ledership.

PUTTING IT ALL TOGETHER

> *There are two ways to exert strength:*
> *one is pushing down,*
> *the other is pulling up.*

—BOOKER T. WASHINGTON, *civil rights activist and educator*

Why would you want to empower your collaborators? For one, it is maybe the most powerful way to enlist collaborators. As the authors of *Enlightened Leadership* note,

> Enlightened leaders know that the hearts and minds of their people can be won when they are working toward a purpose they find worthwhile, are involved in planning and decision-making, and feel appreciated by leadership.[175]

From organizational studies, we know that if members feel they have positive communication with their supervisors, receive specific recognition from those supervisors, and have access to those supervisors, they are more likely to feel empowered.[176] Empowerment must be something you are completely dedicated to. It's a full-time deal. If it seems like the flavor of the month or a "technique" rather than a frame of mind, collaborators will be skeptical. You have to show that empowerment is a foundational mind-set in the organization, by consistently applying its ideals and building structures that support those ideals.

In the previous sections, you learned that for your collaborators to be empowered, they have to know what to do and how to do it, they have to know they have authority, they have to know they are trusted and supported by their leaders, they have to have a safe environment, they have to feel free to communicate openly, and they have to feel that they'll be recognized for their work.

These are not complex ideas, but unfortunately, how many leaders seek consistently to make them reality? How many times have you felt truly empowered in organizations, so that you knew beyond a shadow of a doubt that you could make important decisions or at least participate in those decisions? How many times have you felt that you could be open with your communication, whether positive or negative? How many times have you felt that you trusted everyone in your environment? If you've experienced this, you know why I'm championing empowerment.

Empowerment gives collaborators what they want. I believe that any person in an organization of any kind wants to know and feel that

- They are accepted and understood;
- Their work has meaning;
- They are praised, recognized, and rewarded;
- They have control over their work and careers;
- They have decision-making authority to adequately influence their world, and their opinions count;

- They are needed;
- They belong and are "cared for";
- They are challenged;
- They are supported in that challenge and for their ongoing development;
- They know their expectations, what they are responsible/accountable for, and how they will be measured.

Helping collaborators know and feel these things is the stuff of empowerment. It is the stuff of good leadership. And it is your duty. You are here to help them grow, to help them achieve higher levels of motivation, to support them, to pull them up rather than push them down. As a leader I never feel satisfied until my collaborators can go through the list above and respond with agreement and excitement.

As a leader you must inspire your members to feel empowered, inject as much positive emotion as possible, and dispel fears of failure.[177] The more positive emotion you instill within your collaborators, the likelier they are to have a sense of self-efficacy, the kind of "can-do" attitude that marks many successful organizations. Empowered members of organizations often feel a high sense of self-efficacy, which can be described this way:

> People with high perceived self-efficacy … approach difficult tasks as challenges to be mastered rather than threats to be avoided. They develop interest in what they do, set challenges for themselves, and sustain strong commitments to them. They concentrate on how to perform successfully rather than on disruptive personal concerns when they encounter problems. They attribute their failures to lack of knowledge or skill, faulty strategies, or insufficient effort, all of which are remediable. They redouble their efforts in the face of obstacles and soon recover their self-assurance after setbacks. This outlook sustains motivation, reduces stress, and lowers vulnerability to depression.[178]

Leaders who help others achieve these kinds of states are truly empowering. They are transformational. And they are servants. What more inspiring act can a person do than help others achieve a sense of self-efficacy as described above? As a leader, that's exactly what you do when you empower others.

Leadership Self-Check Questions

Ask yourself:

- Are the decisions and changes I'm making helping others to be wiser, freer, more autonomous, and healthier and to achieve higher levels of motivation?

- Am I being overly controlling?

- Are collaborators able to make decisions and actions that affect their lives and organization?

- Do they have the proper knowledge, skills, abilities, and information to be able to make informed decisions and effectively complete tasks?

- Do they have access to information and educational opportunities?

- Are they encouraged to experiment and participate?

- Do they take the perspective of owners?

- Do they feel they can trust me?

- Do they feel they are supported by me and by organizational structures?

- Are they recognized and rewarded for all their contributions?

Ask collaborators:

- Do you have decision-making authority to adequately influence your world and to feel that your opinions count?

- Do you feel that I trust and support you in making decisions on your own?

- What can I do to increase the sense of community here?

- What can I do to help build a culture of trust, experimentation, and open communication?

- Do you feel needed, accepted, and understood?

- Does your work have meaning?

- Do you feel that you control your career?

- Do you feel that you belong and are cared for?

- Are you challenged enough?

- Are you supported in that challenge and for your on-going development?

- Do you know what your expectations are, what you are responsible/accountable for, and how you will be measured?

CHAPTER SIX

EVALUATE

Today's solutions may well become tomorrow's problems, and effective leaders and organizations are constantly engaged in reflection and self-evaluation.

—SARA E. MELENDEZ, *The Leader of the Future*

I f the word "lead" means "to guide," then one of your primary responsibilities as a leader is to make sure you are on the right path. You have to make sure you are going in the right direction and helping others make the journey in good health. Evaluating your journey, which includes the direction, your ways of doing things, and the people on the trip, is a fundamental responsibility of your role as a leader. This chapter will help you ask important questions along the leadership journey, to make sure you arrive where you want to go. The following sections will help you evaluate (1) your vision, (2) your ethics and performance, and (3) your collaborators' progress.

Evaluate the Vision

Leaders constantly need to evaluate the vision that has been created.[179] You are responsible for your collaborators and where they end up. If, as a servant leader, you hope to help them achieve a state in which they are freer, wiser, more autonomous, and likelier to be servants themselves, you need to be very careful where and how you are leading them. This can be done only by evaluating the fundamental reason why you've come together: to seek envisioned changes that reflect mutual purposes. The envisioned changes, or vision, need to be assessed by both parties in the leadership relationship.

Take ample time to answer the questions posed by Burt Nanus in *Visionary Leadership*.[180] Go through the questions by yourself first. Then, after you've reflected on the vision and evaluated it, bring in some of your collaborators. You can conduct a survey, interview, or focus group. Whatever your method, be sure to get a strong sense of whether people know about the vision, believe in it, and take actions to move toward it on a regular basis.

- How well is the organization doing in moving in the desired direction? Are enough changes being made, and is the rate of progress satisfactory?

- Are people committed to the vision, taking it on as their own, and willing to take the initiative and incur prudent risks to achieve the vision?

- Are the goals and priorities of organizational units, as well as of new projects and program proposals, consistent with the vision? Have new options opened up?

- Are the organization's structures, processes, plans, reward systems, and policies consistent with the vision?

- Do people feel they are pushing the boundaries of their field, that they are "where the action is?" Are they optimistic and enthusiastic about the organization's prospects?

- Are people communicating and cooperating in the accomplishment of the vision, and are they being recognized for their participation in such activities?

- Are influential managers championing the vision, and is there evidence of confidence in leadership?
- Is the culture supportive of the vision, or at least moving in that direction?
- Has the organization been innovative enough in implementing the vision?

After you have evaluated the responses to these questions, you may or may not have to alter the vision. In some cases you may have to start from scratch. For example, if you've been chasing a vision for two years and find that it is no longer representative of mutual purposes, you may have to formulate a new vision. Indeed, visions change over time because so do interests, needs, purposes, and environments. As a leader you have to be aware of these changes and adapt appropriately. At the same time, be careful not to cycle through visions constantly. Few things are worse than being part of an organization that changes its direction too often. Its members feel disjointed, directionless, and disconnected. Your vision should stand the test of time if (1) mutual purposes were built in from the beginning and (2) the vision considers the information in chapter two.

There will be conflict and unease as you progress with your vision. There will always be hesitation, doubt, fear, and distrust in any effort at change. Collaborators will question the path, voice their concerns, and even stand in your group's way if they feel compelled to do so. In the face of these challenges, leaders must accept alternative views, because a voice of dissent is a voice of opportunity to explore new avenues. If you hear such feedback, you are succeeding at creating an open environment of communication and collaboration. As John Gardner notes, "The ideal is leadership strong enough to propose clear directions, and followers strong enough to criticize and amend—and finally enough community of purpose to resolve disputes and move on."[181]

Evaluate Your Ethics and Performace

Leaders and followers have the responsibility and the duty to make ethical judgments concerning the changes they intend for organizations and societies.

—Joseph Rost, *Leadership for the Twenty-First Century*

A survey by James Kouzes and Barry Posner of 1,500 top executives in twenty countries found that "ethics are rated most highly among the personal characteristics needed by the ideal CEO,"[182] yet more than half of the American public believes that our corporate executives are dishonest and that our business leaders' ethical practices merit at best a grade of C.[183] I suspect that this number is significantly higher (and the grade lower) now that the Enron debacle and subsequent corporate scandals have grabbed the headlines. Indeed, at no other time in history has our corporate landscape been so littered with the detritus of corruption and deceit. The many problems facing our nation's businesses in the coming years will either be amplified or dealt with head-on, depending on how ethical our leaders are.

John D. Rockefeller Jr. once said, "I believe that every right implies a responsibility; every opportunity, an obligation; every possession, a duty."[184] Similarly, leaders have the responsibility, obligation, and duty to be ethical. The challenge within this statement is brought to the fore by this commonly asked question: what is "ethics"?

Definitions of "ethics" seem to lie in two camps. Some theorists assert that the word is defined by "how we treat each other, every day, person to person."[185] Rushworth Kidder, a prominent writer and consultant on ethics, says,

> Ethics, after all, is all about the concept of "ought." It is not about what you have to do because regulation compels it (like paying to ride the train) or nature requires it (like eating or sleeping). It's

about what you ought to do—have an obligation
to do—because it is "right."[186]

These observations may be the most useful conceptualization of ethics when applying the term to leadership. The
first definition above takes into account the human side
of ethics in leadership by asking, "Do we treat each other
ethically?" The second considers the purpose side of ethics
in leadership by asking, "Is what we are striving for, and
how we are seeking to achieve it, what we ought to be doing? Is it right?" These two considerations of ethics in leadership—human and purpose[187]—are of vital importance,
and an apt way to frame our leadership choices.

The Human Side of Ethics in Leadership

To treat our collaborators ethically, we need to make sure
we are (1) serving their interests and (2) not abusing power.

The first idea reminds us that as servants to others, leaders need to be honest, fair, and acting in their collaborators'
best interests. According to ethicist Norman E. Bowie, ac-
tors (leaders) are required to take into account the impact
of their actions on others. How will what you do affect
others? If it is negative, should you do it? As Al Gini points
out in *Leading Organizations,* "If and when the interests

of the actor and those affected by the action conflict, the actor should at least consider suspending or modifying his/ her action, and by so doing recognize the interests of the other."[188] In other words, if what you are doing is separate from your collaborators' interests, pause. Think about what you are doing. Think about what people want, and remember mutual purposes. Think about what is right and what you and your collaborators want your leadership legacy to stand for. Then align your actions with others' interests in hopes of serving them.

The second idea reminds us that we should not think of leadership as power *over* but instead as power *with*. As Joseph Rost proposes in *Leadership for the Twenty-First Century*, "When coercive and authoritarian processes are characteristic of a relationship, we can no longer call it leadership."[189] This is because leadership is an influence relationship, not a forced one. People choose to be in the relationship because of their belief that it reflects mutual purposes and that important ends will be achieved, not because you force them to. Collaborators must have the choice whether to be in the relationship and whether and how much to influence the relationship's purposes. According to Rost, the bottom line is, "do people in the relationship (leaders and followers) have freedom of choice, or is choice, for all practical purposes, taken away?"[190]

This idea of not abusing power also means not withholding information, lying, stealing, misdirecting, or subverting others' efforts. I wish we were at a point in leadership where we didn't have to voice such seemingly apparent concepts, but unfortunately, the headlines remind us that there is still work to do here.

These ideas about ethics on the human side of leadership should be pegged to a standard in which leaders can answer only yes to these questions:

- Am I acting in the best interests of my collaborators?
- Do my collaborators have the choice to agree on what they are doing?
- Am I being honest?
- Am I using power in a way that is legal, forthright, and in the best interests of everyone I am influencing?

Ethics in the Purposes of Leadership

While the human side of ethics may seem simple from the previous questions, ethics in the *purposes* of leadership are more complex. The purposes of leadership deal with what the leaders and collaborators are trying to achieve, the end result. It may be a change in policy, attitudes, performance, or the greater society. The difficulty in dealing with the ethics of purposes in leadership can be seen in this question: What decisions and changes are ethical? Think about the issue of abortion. If leaders and collaborators want to keep it legal, is that ethical? Everyone has his or her own idea of what is ethical.

Rushworth Kidder points out in his insightful *How Good People Make Tough Choices* (which should be required reading for all leaders) that many of the choices we face put us in a "right versus right" dilemma. In other words, sometimes the most difficult choices we must make are between two opposing sides that are both reasonable. Kidder notes these examples:

- It is right to extend equal social services to everyone regardless of race or ethnic origin—and right to pay special attention to those whose cultural backgrounds may have deprived them of past opportunities.

- It is right to provide our children with the finest public schools available—and right to prevent the constant upward ratcheting of state and local taxes.

- It is right to take the family on a much-needed vacation—and right to save that money for your children's education.

- It is right to "throw the book" at good employees who make dumb decisions and endanger the firm—and right to have enough compassion to mitigate the punishment and give them another chance.[191]

Many choices that leaders face are just such right-versus-right decisions. Kidder further points out that the *really* tough choices we face often revolve around four dilemmas.

Justice versus mercy. Do we execute a murderer or forgive him and help him rehabilitate? Do we ask a slower group member who is hurting our overall performance to leave, or do we accept and coach him? "The point behind the justice-versus-mercy paradigm is that fairness, equity, and even-handed application of the law often conflict with compassion, empathy, and love."[192]

The short term versus the long term. Do I spend our entire budget on an important project this semester, or hold it for next? Should I bring up an irresolvable conflict with a collaborator now, or bury the issue because I need his support next month? "Short-term versus long-term, or *now versus then*, reflects the difficulties arising when immediate needs or desires run counter to future goals or prospects."[193]

Individual versus community. Do we hoard all the available budget to get our project complete, or share the funds to help another equally important program begin? Should I tell the president I made a mistake that could hurt the company, or protect my career? "The individual-versus-community paradigm can be restated as *us versus them, self versus others,* or *the smaller versus the larger* group."[194]

Truth versus loyalty. When my boss asks about a specific coworker's performance, do I tell her that person is constantly late and upsetting the entire staff, or do I say nothing because that coworker is a friend? Do I tell a woman her husband is cheating on her, or not disclose it because he is my pastor? "Truth versus loyalty can be seen as honesty or integrity versus commitment, responsibility, or promise-keeping."[195]

The point here, of course, is that we face many debates and decisions that are ethically challenging. We recognize that there are tough choices, but how do we make the right ones?

Unfortunately, many people make it sound easy to make the right call. We hear their self-assured counsel of "Don't break the law, lie, cheat, steal, or do harm." Good advice, but too simplistic for many of our difficult decisions. Some laws *must* be broken (think of the civil disobedience movements of Mohandas K. Gandhi and Martin Luther King Jr.). Sometimes we have to silence our voices rather than speak hurtful truths. Sometimes we have to do bad to do good (think of hurting a person's feelings by ending a romantic relationship because doing so protects both people from further pain).

Plenty of organizations and groups have attempted to answer the question "How do we make ethical choices?" Most corporations in the United States and Europe have codes of ethics. So do religions (think Ten Commandments). And so do groups such as the Boy Scouts (the Boy Scout Law) and our doctors (the Hippocratic oath). These codes, laws, and oaths are all efforts to help us "do right."

Philosophers and academics have offered plenty of frameworks for being ethical. In fact, many claim to have found "universal" ethical and moral codes that exist throughout the world. Here are two:

The Moral Rules: A New Rational Foundation for Morality[196]

1. Don't kill
2. Don't cause pain
3. Don't disable
4. Don't deprive others of freedom or opportunity
5. Don't deprive others of pleasure
6. Don't deceive
7. Keep your promises
8. Don't cheat
9. Obey the law
10. Do your duty

Global Responsibility: In Search of a New World Ethic[197]
1. Don't kill
2. Don't lie
3. Don't steal
4. Don't practice immorality
5. Respect your parents and love your children

In addition to these universal codes, Kidder has proposed "universal values," which, if respected and practiced, keep us ethical and moral. In *Shared Values for a Troubled World: Conversations with Men and Women of Conscience,* he details these values:[198]

- Love
- Truth
- Fairness
- Freedom
- Unity
- Tolerance
- Responsibility
- Respect for life

Question-answer paradigms have also been created to help us make ethical decisions. Utilitarian ethics say, "Do what brings the most good to the greatest number of people." Rules ethics say, "Do what you would want everyone else in the world to do from now on in this situation."

Contract ethics say, "Do what the group you are working with would agree is the ethical standard." Golden Rule ethics say, "Do what you would want others to do to you." Caretaker rules say, "Do whatever will not harm." Other question-answer paradigms say, "Do what you would be least ashamed of if your decision appeared in the morning paper," or "Do what your parent/grandfather/mentor/idol would do." I often tell leaders to ask themselves and their collaborators a whole battery of such questions as they go about choosing the "right path."

These thoughts are all valuable, and I encourage you to read everything you can on ethics and form your own codes, values, and questions—not just for use in leadership roles, but for your everyday life.

The only fixed ideas I have about ethics in leadership are rooted in the belief that we must act for the common good. Ethics in leadership isn't about "individual" ethics—simply the leader's or collaborators' ethics. It isn't about the leader's and collaborators' mutually developed ethics, either. These are components but not the whole. According to Rost, ethics in leadership must be thought of as a concept of civic virtue, "the elemental notion that all of our goods as individuals and groups are bound up in the common good, or, to put it another way, that all of our self- and group interests are bound up in the public interest."[199] Ethics in leadership is thus about the ethics of the greater community and society we live in.

It isn't my intention to develop a framework for ethics or to describe what ethics should be in society. It is my intention, though, to get you thinking about ethics at a broader level than your narrow personal beliefs. By serving a common good, that of a larger public interest, I believe that leaders are ethical. Indeed, I believe that anyone who is called a "leader" *must* be ethical. For example, as I discussed earlier, many authors describe Hitler as a leader. Under this guide's conceptualization of leadership and its emphasis on evaluating ethics, though, Hitler was no leader. He did not serve the greater good. He did not ethically question what he was doing. A leader cannot simply ask, "Is this good for me and for some of my collaborators?" A leader must ask, "Is this right for the public interest, society, and humanity at large?"

The question of ethics relating to the purposes of leadership is difficult to wrestle with. I believe it's important to stick to a few values derived from servant leadership when considering your role as a leader. Servant leadership asks simply, "Are the decisions and changes you are making helping others (the public interest, society, humanity at large) grow, become wiser, freer, more autonomous, healthier, and better able to achieve a higher sense of motivation and morality?" This may or may not be a measure of ethics. Nevertheless, it is an important consideration if you subscribe to the ideals of servant leadership.

In order to help you bring the ethical considerations in leadership together in practice, let's take a look at a review that found that leaders could be ethical or unethical in five areas: exercising powers, creating visions, communicating with followers, intellectually stimulating followers, developing followers, and adhering to moral standards.[200]

Exercising Power

Ethical leaders exercise power in "socially constructive ways to serve others," not to serve themselves, manipulate others, or "win at all costs."[201] They are not Enron-style leaders. They are responsible, truthful, and accountable. As discussed above, they also exercise power *with* instead of power *over*. Leaders need to give their collaborators choices and information so that they can make intelligent decisions. They need to exercise influence, not top-down, dictator-style power.

Creating Visions

Ethical leaders create visions that are responsive to collaborators' needs and interests and that allow collaborators to "actively contribute to and develop the vision further so that it is shared."[202] This ideal—that leaders need to include the voice of their collaborators—was discussed in chapter two. Leaders need to allow others to shape, alter, and act on purposes they believe in.

Communicating with Collaborators

Ethical leaders ask a lot of questions and avidly seek collaborators' input and ideas. They "listen to the ideas, needs, aspirations, and wishes of followers"[203] in hopes of figuring out how best to serve them. They ask for open communication in which people readily give feedback. Indeed, most leaders don't get enough feedback, partly because they don't ask, and partly because their followers fear giving it.[204] Ethical leaders, though, accept and promote an open feedback environment, where their decisions can be challenged and questioned and where they can learn from their mistakes. Also, ethical leaders never leave collaborators in the dark—collaborators are well informed and have an ongoing, two-way communicative relationship with leaders. A heavy responsibility of leaders is to communicate with collaborators openly in order to create shared realities and mutual purposes, and ethical leaders do just that.

Stimulating Followers Intellectually

Ethical leaders encourage different ways of thinking. It's not "my way or the highway." They promote an environment open to diverse ideas and new ways of thinking. Collaborators are asked to consider diverse viewpoints and opinions. They are asked to challenge basic assumptions in the status quo, as well as the norms of interaction among their leaders and themselves. Intellectual stimulation—the degree to which leaders promote new ways of viewing situations or problems and conducting deeper analysis of those problems—is highly related to exactly what transformational leaders do.[205]

Ethical leaders also allow their people to use their signature strengths. Collaborators are allowed to do and be what they are good at and are positioned in areas they are passionate about.

Developing Followers

Ethical leaders "express confidence in their followers' capabilities to achieve the vision" and "focus on developing people with whom they interact to higher levels of ability, motivation, and morality."[206] This point mirrors James McGregor Burns's ideas about transformational leadership. By empowering and encouraging their collaborators, leaders are responsible for helping collaborators grow and become wiser, more autonomous, and closer to their ideal selves. Leaders provide training, opportunity, feedback, mentoring, and coaching.

Using Moral Standards

Ethical leaders have a well-grounded sense of what is right and what is wrong, and they always favor the right. "They promote a vision that inspires followers to accomplish objectives that are constructive for both the organization *and* society."[207] Leaders have to ask tough questions about what is appropriate for the common good, the public interest, and society at large. Leaders use high moral standards in taking care of others rather than hurting or manipulating them. They are truthful and seek to help others, rather than being deceitful in an attempt to help themselves. In all, leaders' actions and decisions can be said to be centered on civic virtue and the common good.

The beginning of this century may well be remembered as a time when business leaders checked their ethics at the door when they entered their offices. The corporate scandals that have recently rocked the country will be the "don't do this" business case studies of the next decade. In other words, ethical violations leave lasting legacies. So ask yourself now, "What legacy will I leave?"

EVALUATE COLLABORATOS' PROGRESS

*Why do we monitor people
rather than mentor people?*

—DR. ANN MCGEE COOPER, *Insights on Leadership*

A vital role of leaders is to evaluate their collaborators' progress in hopes of helping them grow. People look to their leaders to see how they're doing, and it is a leader's obligation to let them know.

Evaluating collaborators comes as close to management as leadership gets, but it is fundamentally different. Management's purposes in evaluation can be said to be a tool to make employees more efficient, more controllable, more aligned to a framework of "what works" so that the *organization* can benefit and grow. A leader's purposes in evaluation have to do with helping benefit the *individual* so that the individual can grow. Managers evaluate people because those people are *subordinates* and it is the manager's duty to *control* them. Leaders evaluate people because those people are their *collaborators* and it is the leader's duty to *serve* them.

These distinctions are important because they dictate a fundamental shift in evaluating others. In leadership there is a realistic and uplifting move from criticism and judgment to embracing, supporting, and encouraging all those you attempt to influence. Leaders support, encourage, and praise collaborators more often than they criticize and give negative feedback, because positive feedback is generally more productive and effective than negative feedback.[208]

It is not my intention to prescribe a set of criteria on how to evaluate collaborators' progress. Criteria must be specific to the context you are leading in. It would be difficult to set up the same criteria for members' success in a church as for members' success in the military. The only common-criteria theme I can distinguish would result in questions that revolve around the themes of servant leadership: Are collaborators growing, becoming wiser and more autonomous, achieving a higher sense of motivation and morality, and themselves becoming leaders?

Instead, this section focuses more on how to engage others as you evaluate them. While the criteria for evaluating progress can change from context to context, as can the methods of evaluation, leaders know that they must engage collaborators in a way that helps them change and grow.

Leaders realize that evaluations don't change people; relationships do. Carl Rogers, the humanistic psychologist who founded client-centered therapy, understood this concept well. He found that to effect change in people and help them grow as individuals, the relationship between therapist and client should be based on (1) unconditional positive regard, (2) genuineness, and (3) empathy.[209] These ideals are important in the leader-collaborator relationship. Collaborators must feel that leaders view them with unconditional positive regard, that they see collaborators as inherently valuable no matter what condition they are in or what behaviors they are enacting. Collaborators need to feel that leaders are genuine with them, that they are honest and forthright with their communication and observations. Finally, collaborators must sense that leaders are empathetic, that leaders can sense what they are feeling and understand them in their current reality.

Leaders recognize that people are not problems; they are priorities. If a collaborator is having difficulties, leaders don't seek to "punish" him or her. Here is what one author wrote about punishment:

> The quickest and simplest way to reduce the frequency of an undesired behavior is to apply some form of punishing consequence. But the reduction in the frequency of misbehavior is the

short-term consequence. The use of punishment produces side effects and long-term consequences—anger, apathy, resentment, frustration—that end up being far more costly than whatever the original misbehavior might have been.[210]

Leaders seek to help collaborators grow, to support and guide them, not punish them. Sometimes, of course, this means "getting real" and giving negative feedback. Leaders are often reluctant to give negative feedback, though, and when they do "they distort their feedback and make it more positive than it should be."[211] This is where Rogers's ideas about genuineness come into play. Leaders have to give feedback, both positive and negative. They have to be candid and honest with their observations. If this honesty is coming from a supportive standpoint, it most likely won't be received as negative or insulting.

With this genuineness, Rogers recommends being empathetic. Robert Greenleaf would seem to agree as he reminds us, "Individuals grow taller when those who lead them empathize and when they are accepted for what they are, even though their performance may be judged critically in terms of what they are capable of doing."[212]

Leaders need to be careful with their assumptions about poor performance, though. Many collaborator "problems" happen because (1) the collaborators don't have the knowledge or skill to do their job, (2) they don't understand their responsibilities, or (3) they haven't received feedback and think they're doing their jobs correctly.[213] You need to make sure that, as discussed in the last chapter, people have the education, information, and skills they need to do a job and receive feedback consistently.

Feedback should be frequent, timely, and specific and should include praise or developmental direction (an action plan).[214] If collaborators do something you disagree with, let them know as soon as possible, be specific about what they did, listen to their comments, give praise where appropriate, and, if necessary, offer them ideas about what they could do differently in the future. With these ideas in mind, I believe the purpose of feedback is to help people (1) become *aware* of what is happening, (2) realize they are *accountable* for their behavior and role within the organization, and (3) decide on a course of *action* to take in the future.

All this is done only in an effort to help others grow and become wiser, and must be done with unconditional positive regard, genuineness, and empathy. Feedback can cause people to become resentful, defensive, and less committed,[215] so be sure to champion these supportive and attentive ideals.

If you hurt someone with evaluative and critical statements, stop. Apologize. Don't make excuses for doing it; promise not to do it again. Say, "I'm sorry I hurt you; I won't do that again. There's no excuse. Again, I'm sorry." If someone seeks reasons for your critical words, say, "I just wasn't acting responsibly; I wasn't in the right frame of mind. But that's not an excuse for what I did. I'm sorry, and it won't happen again."

Again, you need to focus on your relationship with your collaborators while evaluating their progress. You need to be a care*giver*, not a care*taker*. Evaluating collaborators' progress must be handled from the viewpoint of the servant who helps them grow and achieve a higher sense of motivation and morality.

The evaluative role of a leader is a challenging one. Assessing the vision, ethics, and progress of collaborators is taxing but absolutely crucial. If your vision is not representative of mutual purposes and does not gain collaborator commitment, the leadership process stops. If your ethics are self-serving, dishonest, coercive, and damaging to humanity, the leadership process should stop. And finally, if your collaborators' progress is not positive and they do not grow as individuals, *they* will make the leadership process stop. Leaders are skillful evaluators, and those who believe in servant leadership are able not only to evaluate but also to build stronger visions, ethical standards, and worthy collaborators from those assessments.

LEADERSHIP SELF-CHECK QUESTIONS

Ask yourself:

- Are people committed to the vision, taking it on as their own, and willing to take the initiative and incur prudent risks to achieve the vision?

- Am I treating people ethically and doing things that are ethical?

- Are the decisions and changes I'm making helping others to be wiser, freer, more autonomous, and healthier and to achieve higher levels of morality?

- Am I giving unconditional positive regard, genuineness, and empathy?

- Have my collaborators made progress?

- Did they know what they were supposed to do and how to do it?

- Have they had enough feedback?

- Am I being supportive?

- Is this the way I would like to be treated?

- Am I being open and direct?

- Am I tactful?

- Have I asked for their point of view?

- What were the conditions my collaborators were working under?

- Have I been available to help?

Ask collaborators:

- What am I not doing that you want me to do so that you can succeed?

- Do I listen enough?

- Are you getting the feedback from me that you need to perform at your highest levels?

- Are we all heading in the right direction and doing what it takes to get there?

- Am I helping?

- Am I clear about what I expect from everyone?

- Do I support you enough?

- How does everyone feel about what we're doing now?

- What can I do to better track our progress?

CHAPTER SEVEN

Encourage

*Leaders we admire do not place themselves at the
center; they place others there.
They do not seek the attention of people;
they give it to others.*

—James Kouzes and Barry Posner, *Credibility*

The previous chapters had many tips and step-by-step considerations that leaders can use to become more effective servants. This chapter has no step-by-step ideas. It can't. There is no simplified way to make others feel encouraged, lifted, supported, or loved. Somehow, though, this is what leaders do. As Kouzes and

Posner point out, when you ask people about how their leaders make them feel, you hear words like "motivated," "inspired," "supported," "respected," "proud," and "valued." You don't hear words like "stupid," "sad," or "intimidated."[216] This observation leads me to ask, "Where did we ever get the idea that we can help people become more by making them feel bad?"

Indeed, under some old ideas of leadership (i.e., management), human traits like uniqueness, free will, and creativity are seen as problems because they mean that people cannot be controlled.[217] In servant leadership, though, these traits are not seen as *problems;* they are championed as *priorities.* Servant leaders seek to encourage collaborators' uniqueness in the interest of helping them grow into healthier, wiser, freer, and more autonomous human beings.

Encouraging collaborators in their quest to achieve goals and become better human beings is the *central activity* leaders must commit to. And evidence shows that it is necessary. The authors of *Charismatic Leadership in Organizations* found, "Without the leader's affirmation, [collaborators] can feel that they are underperforming and even failing."[218] Not encouraging or affirming collaborators can leave them feeling powerless, unappreciated, disrespected, used, lost, and unmotivated. On the other hand, encouraging collaborators has tremendous and vital benefits. Leaders achieve high collaborator motivation by raising their self-esteem and self-worth.[219] Credibility, respect, and loyalty "are earned by appreciating others, affirming others, and developing others."[220] The more positive feedback people receive from their leaders, the more satisfied they are[221] and the better they perform.[222] When followers feel encouraged, appreciated, and supported, they are likelier to be proud of what they're doing, work hard, feel as though they are members of the team, link their identities to their endeavors, gain commitment, and grow as individuals.

Your role as a leader is to take every opportunity available to encourage, support, and affirm your collaborators. This is not "touchy-feely" or esoteric. Encouragement makes the leadership float. It is the architecture of motivation. It is very much a science of extending empowerment to the emotional well-being of your collaborators. As discussed in chapter five, you need to recognize and reward their efforts. You need to praise them publicly and affirm them in private conversations, too. You need to lift them up when they have fallen, when they have lost hope and direction. Leaders encourage collaborators to keep forging ahead despite small tumbles. Sometimes they just point out the way. Sometimes they walk with them. Sometimes they join hands. And sometimes, in the darkest moments, leaders help carry them until they can walk on their own.

John Gardner, one of our country's most inspiring leaders and leadership theorists, says, "The reservoir of unused human talent and energy is vast, and learning to tap that reservoir more effectively is one of the exciting tasks ahead for humankind."[223] Leaders, through encouragement, help people tap their personal reserves. They help bring the best of people's talent and personality into the service of achieving important changes.

As I said above, there is no step-by-step process for encouraging others. It is a human activity that is, and should be, without a manual. The best I can do is offer you a glimpse into two profound personal experiences: one when I was a student, and the other when I was a teacher.

A STUDENT'S LEADER

In high school I was a misguided missile. I was running around in twenty-four directions at once. My enormous energy was unfocused. And, like many people with more energy than focus, I ran into trouble—lots of it. I revolted against any kind of authority or rule that came my way. It's not that I was disrespectful of others or got bad grades.

I was just *loud,* always pushing the limits and constantly questioning the rules.

When I was a sophomore, all these traits converged in one incident. My parents had decided we were going to France for a month-long family reunion so that we could meet my mother's side of the family for the first time. They picked the month of March to go, the very middle of the school semester, because it was the only time both sides of the family could conveniently meet. When I asked my school counselor and my teachers if it would be possible to get the time off, they said yes. They knew I was a good student and could make up the homework. Several teachers would even make accommodations for such an experience. My French teacher would let me skip workbook assignments as long as I gave all her classes a presentation about my trip. My art teacher would allow me to miss the days as long as I brought back photographs of the historic museums and several pieces of framed art and gave a presentation on each.

This was the first semester of a new ten-day absence policy, though, and as soon as the administration found out about the trip, they were up in arms to "set an example" about how important this policy was. I was going to miss twenty-one days of school, and that was unacceptable for me to get an "appropriate" education. The principal told my parents I couldn't go. So they went to the assistant superintendent and then the superintendent of public schools. They said no. So my parents decided to appeal to the school board. The board met, then met with my dad and said no. Then I got *loud*.

I wrote a blasting commentary to my local newspaper, and it was the featured guest column in the front section. After detailing how I could have made up the classes, and the process of how the school board had come to the decision that the trip was a no-go, I wrote,

> As Mark Twain said, "Never let school get in the way of an education." I am going on the trip. I am willing to lose credit, take summer school, and sacrifice my junior year for makeup. After all, it's France.

> I feel that the school system and the school board failed to realize the educational aspects of the trip, and also failed one of its prominent students.

> I believe the school board should get its head out of the clouds and accept the fact that education not only lies in a teacher's oral presentations, reading, and book work, but also in *seeing* and *experiencing*.[224]

Public outcry was immediate. People flooded the administration with phone calls. Soon the school board decided to have another meeting. They would let their final decision be known at a public meeting two weeks later. Anticipation for the decision was huge; the crowd at the meeting was said to be one of the largest in school board history.

For some reason I can't remember now, my parents couldn't make the meeting, but I was there. So were half my classmates. And so were the television cameras. In a dramatic five-to-two decision justified by the need to curb absenteeism and maintain the integrity of the new policy, the final answer was no. My first moment on television shows me sitting amid the roar of jeers for the decision, alone and crying.

The tears of sorrow soon turned to tears of joy as I met family in France. The trip forever changed me. When I got back home, I ended up presenting in both my art and French classes, even though I was no longer a student at the school. I was even asked at one point to leave the building. Many of the teachers at the school saw one presentation or another. Many of them came to see my slide show, but none of them had come with me to fight the school board. I was dejected and ready to walk away from school forever.

And then a leader entered my life. Linda Ballew, an English teacher who also headed the school's student newspaper, heard about my slides and photographs of France. She also remembered my article in the paper. Somehow we met, and she told me I was a strong writer and that my article had ruffled some feathers that needed ruffling. She said my art teacher told her my photographs were well composed. Most importantly, she told me I had potential. Then she asked me to join the student newspaper the next semester when I returned to school.

I told her I might not come back next semester. I told her I was angry as hell at the administration. Of course, I was mostly just hurt, disappointed, and alone. And with what would be the standard of all her interactions with students, she listened, comforted me, and inspired me. I was too good not to come back, she said. I had too much potential and too many talents not to use them in a creative endeavor. She said I was not the type to quit anything and that I had plenty of good to do at the school.

The next semester I went back.

I honestly don't know if she even remembers the short conversation, but I do and always will.

That next year, Linda took a ragtag team of students and flooded their hearts with hope and inspiration. She led us to being hopeful that we could be the best newspaper in the country. Despite the resources the bigger schools had, she said we could compete because we were creative, strong, and intelligent students. She inspired us to raise our efforts to the next level. She guided us but let us guide the direction of the paper.

Every weekend and every late night spent working on our paper, Linda was there. She helped us in every aspect of journalism because she had gained expertise in every aspect. She showed us how to analyze our competition and strive to improve on our last issue. She guided us to come together as a team, supporting one another and building on one another's strengths. With steadfastness and compassion, she helped us become more competent and confident. In more than one way Linda helped us become better human beings.

That year we won "best of show" at the national Journalism Education Association convention. We were number one in the country. A small school from Montana, beating the big boys because we were injected with hope, inspiration, and constant nourishing encouragement from the best leader I've met in my life so far.

Over the next year and a half, Linda took me under her wing, as she did everyone, and lifted me to become wiser, healthier, more autonomous, and more motivated. I won national and regional first- and second-place awards for photography, layout and design, news writing, and investigative reporting. I even became a leader myself when I was named managing editor. More importantly, I became a servant to others, just as Linda had taught me, helping others achieve the best that they could, lifting them up with hope, inspiration, support, love, and never-ending encouragement.

ANOTHER STUDENT'S LEADER?

What Linda had taught me came full circle when I became a public speaking instructor at The University of Montana. I was bubbling over with excitement about being in a position to lift up and educate students. I put full effort into all my classes, reinventing ways public speaking had been taught, and teaching with every ounce of passion I had. But, as often happens with new teachers, toward the end of my first year I became worn out. I had taken on a lot that semester, and suddenly I didn't feel that I was making a difference anymore. And then a leadership opportunity presented itself in an odd place: through a shy, reserved, withdrawn student named Sarah.

At the beginning of the semester Sarah didn't seem like a troubled student. She was at every class. She was on time. But soon she was in trouble. She skipped her first two speeches—she just didn't show up on her assigned days. This alone guaranteed her failure in the course. And yet, even after missing those two crucial days, she showed up on time every day for class. I kept trying to chat with her after class, but so many other students would be asking questions, and Sarah always seemed to slip quietly out of the classroom before I could reach her.

Three weeks before finals week I posted the speaking assignments for the class, listing who would speak on which day. Sarah's name was not on the list. She had never given a speech and had already failed the class, so I didn't include her. A few days later, as I was helping another student during my office hours, I saw Sarah enter the office, looking rather sheepish. She chewed her nails and kicked her feet the entire time she waited for me to finish with the other student.

When at last we spoke, she surprised me with an immediate request: "Brendon, I want to give my finals speech." I was shocked. Not understanding her intentions—and, worse yet, forgetting to be encouraging—I said, "Why would you want to give the speech? You do understand you have failed this course, don't you?"

She said, "I know…I've messed up. But I've come to class every day because you inspire me, and I knew if I kept coming you might help me actually get up there in front of the class. I think I'm ready. I want to try this now, Brendon. You've led me this far; please don't lose faith now. I want to do this for you and the class. I have to do this for *me*."

When she said I had inspired her and "led her," I thought about this guide. I thought about leadership. I thought about Linda Ballew and her strength. I pulled a copy of the speaking schedule out of my binder, put it on the desk, and wrote Sarah's name on the last day of speeches. She stared at her name on the schedule, and when she looked up she had tears in her eyes. She uttered a muffled thank-you and walked out of the office.

We spent the next day talking about what she wanted to accomplish and what I'd like to see her do—our mutual purposes. It would be a quick two weeks of preparation, but I told her I knew she could do it—without ever having seen her speak publicly before. We met every other day. More than half that time was spent reassuring her that she could do it and coaching her to beat away her fears. When her faith stumbled, I did my best to pick her up with hope and encouragement. Whenever she ran out of faith, I repeated this quote from Elisabeth Kübler-Ross:

> When you come to the edge of all the light you
> know and are about to step into the darkness of

the unknown, faith is knowing that one of two things will happen: there will be something solid to stand on, or you'll be taught to fly.[225]

I let her know that if her words stumbled, she would find another sentence to stand on, or somehow, in that unbearable moment of uncertainty, she would be given the words to fly by. After two weeks of personally coaching her, I honestly didn't know if she would show up on her speech day.

But she did. When she approached the podium, nearly half the class turned to me with questioning looks, as if to say, "Is she really going to talk?" Sarah worked her way through ten minutes. During the middle of her speech she seemed to lose her words for a few seconds—by the expression on her face, a painfully long time. Then one of her classmates encouraged softly, "You've got it, Sarah; it's okay." She found her words and finished the speech.

If I had graded her formally, I imagine she would have gotten a C-minus. But as she finished, the class responded with resounding applause, as though she had given the most stirring speech in history. She walked back to her desk as people were still clapping, hooting, and giving her praise. Her best friend glowed and said with great pride,

"You *did* it, Sarah." She then reached over and gave her a hug. The feeling in the class was exuberant, and at the end of the day several people walked past Sarah and praised her inspiring performance.

As the last of the class filtered out of the classroom and I was putting folders in my bag, I caught Sarah out of the corner of my eye, standing alone at the doorway. Turning, I saw tears welling in her eyes. What she said to me next were the most wonderful words I've heard in my life, and reaffirmed to me the reasons we do this thing called leadership. Struggling to hold back tears and the overwhelming emotions she must have felt, Sarah whispered to me as she turned and left, "Thank you, Brendon. You are the only person who ever told me I had any potential."

THE HEART OF LEADERSHIP

If leadership is rooted in service, as discussed in the introduction and throughout this guide, then service is rooted in encouragement. Leaders help unlock the strengths and passions of people through encouragement. Like me in the first story and Sarah in the second, people need to be reminded they are worthy and capable. There are so many people out there who need you. They need your help to reach their purpose. They need to be encouraged by words of inspiration and conversations of hope. They need to be told they have potential. They need support when they falter, and assurance that they can make the next step.

You need to serve this role, because that is how you will ultimately be measured. Dr. Jack Weber, professor of management at The University of Virginia, has said,

> The bottom line is that leadership shows up in the inspired actions of others. We traditionally have assessed leaders themselves. But maybe we should assess leadership by the degree to which people around leaders are inspired.[226]

Maybe it *is* time that leaders were judged on how encouraged and inspired their collaborators are. Maybe it is time leaders were judged by the level to which their collaborators are transformed into achieving higher levels of motivation and morality, as Burns describes with transformational leadership.

Certainly, accomplishments are not the best assessment of leaders. Because the truth is, all the awards I won in high school journalism aren't a reflection of Linda Ballew's leadership. And Sarah's speech itself is certainly not the best testament to my leadership. What it took for us to achieve those accomplishments was the encouragement provided by leaders who believed in us, inspired us, and transformed us by uncovering our unique potential. For if it weren't for the hope, inspiration, and dedicated and constant encouragement, those accomplishments would never have taken place.

Leaders are, in essence, masters of encouragement. They don't encourage to accomplish; they encourage to bring out the best in people and to remind them that they are capable. Nobel laureate William Faulkner, author of *The Sound and the Fury* and *As I Lay Dying,* once said this about writers, which I believe applies directly to leaders:

> It is his privilege to help man endure by lifting his heart, by reminding him of the courage and honor and hope and pride and compassion and pity and sacrifice which have been the glory of his past.[227]

And, I would add, by reminding him of the courage and honor and hope and pride and compassion that *could be* the glory of his future.

Leadership Self-Check Questions

Ask yourself:

- Am I giving attention to my collaborators? Are they placed at the center?

- Do I focus on their strengths and openly praise those strengths?

- What do I do, or can I do, to give them hope and inspiration?

- Are the decisions and changes I'm making helping others to be wiser, freer, more autonomous, and healthier and to achieve higher levels of morality?

- Am I giving unconditional positive regard, genuineness, and empathy?

- What have I said, or could I say, to help my collaborators realize that they have potential?

- Is this the way I would like to be treated?

- Have I been available to help, support, inspire, love, and encourage?

Ask collaborators:

- What am I not doing that you want me to do so that you can succeed?

- Do I listen enough?

- Am I helping?

- What can I do to help you achieve your full potential?

- Do I support you enough?

- Do you feel valued around here?

- Do you feel that you belong?

- Is the work you are doing meaningful to you?

- Is everything in your life going okay right now? Can I help with anything?

- What makes you feel most excited about our endeavor?

- How can we help others feel that they are doing a great job?

- What do others around here need in order to feel more excited, motivated, and inspired?

BEYOND THE CLASSROOM

It is meaningless to talk about leadership
unless we believe that individuals
can make a difference
in the lives of others.

—JAMES KOUZES AND BARRY POSNER, *Credibility*

As Joseph Rost pointed out in *Leadership for the Twenty-First Century*, leadership itself "is not the answer to all the ills of our societies or their institutions and organizations."[228] Unfortunately, the term "leadership" has been thrown around by the media and society as *the* answer to all the challenges confronting us. We

211

hear the echoing voices of people saying, "Our leaders will show us the way." As I hope you have found throughout this guide, the answer doesn't lie just in our leaders. Like leadership itself, the answers to the challenges confronting us lie in our collective decisions and actions.

At the same time, leaders are tremendously powerful in helping us confront these challenges. It would be naive to say that the leaders of our organizations, communities, and households do not dramatically influence the direction of society. The noted political leader and leadership theorist John Gardner says,

> Leaders have a significant role in creating the state of mind that is the society. They can serve as symbols of the moral unity of the society. They can express the values that hold the society together. Most important, they can conceive and articulate goals that lift people out of their petty preoccupations, carry them above the conflicts that tear a society apart, and unite them in pursuit of objectives worthy of their best efforts.[229]

Look again at the words Gardner uses. Leaders are "symbols" who can "express...conceive and articulate goals" in order to lift, carry, and unite. These words are poignant and inseparable from the concept of leadership.

This guide has attempted to present other words that should be inseparable from the concept:

- service
- relationships
- mutual purposes
- collaborators
- embodiment
- empowerment
- ethics
- encouragement

These words and associated concepts can't be separated from leadership. Leadership will always be the process of leaders and followers coming together through an influence relationship and seeking envisioned changes that reflect their mutual purposes. It will always be rooted in service and enacted by ethical leaders through empowerment and encouragement.

People will always look to leaders to face challenges. Hopefully, they will first look inward and to each side. Then, if needed, they can look to leaders. It would be wonderful if people took responsibility for themselves and somehow were able to come together and collectively move toward important purposes. I am optimistic that we as a society are coming closer to that golden state. And yet, even if we achieve this ideal, the authors of *Credibility* remind us,

> But people still want and need leadership. They just want leaders who hold to an ethic of service and are genuinely respectful of the intelligence and contributions of their constituents. They want leaders who will put principles ahead of politics and other people before self-interests.[230]

Indeed, people will look to their leaders, and we hope those leaders will be like the ones described above. We hope they will serve us. We hope they will respect us. We hope they will stand for principles. These are the leaders who will be effective in the future. As Richard Beckhard, an editor of *The Leader of the Future,* believes,

> Truly effective leaders in the years ahead will have personas determined by strong values and belief in the capacity of individuals to grow. They will have an image of society in which they would like their organizations and themselves to live. They will be visionary, they will believe strongly that they can and should be shaping the future, and

they will act on these beliefs through their personal behavior.[231]

This guide's intention has been to help you see how to enact these beliefs of "personal behavior." The framework offered, E⁶, was designed to help you think of behavior focused on helping others grow, and envisioning and seeking to shape the future. To be truly effective, leaders of the future will have to follow these principles, and a way to do so is with the E⁶ framework. By envisioning the future, enlisting others to help shape that vision, embodying the ideals you seek and preach, empowering others so they can seek to attain that future, evaluating progress and ethics, and encouraging others to sustain the journey and become stronger, leaders become effective.

The day will come—indeed, it may already be upon you—when others look to you to lead. How will you lead? What will you stand for? How will you treat others? These questions and other important ones posed in previous chapters, and their answers, will determine your effectiveness and the level to which you serve your collaborators.

I believe that if we, as students, begin this century forging a stronger society built on the ideals of service, collaboration, and empowerment, we can address the important challenges of today and become the inspiring architects of our age. And I believe we need to start now so that in the latter years of our lives we won't have to look back on missed opportunities and feel the dreaded emotions epitomized by the words "We wait too long."

NOTE TO READERS

IF YOU HAVE COMMENTS about this book, or a leadership experience you would like to share with the author, please e-mail brendon@brendonburchard.com.

To book a speaking event with the author or to inquire about purchasing *The Student Leadership Guide* in bulk, e-mail staff@TheStudentLeadershipGuide.com.

To learn about Brendon Burchard's books, speeches, and seminars, visit www.BrendonBurchard.com.

ENDNOTES

INTRODUCTION

1   Kirkpatrick and Locke, 1991.

2 Jeffries, 1998, 36

3 See Bass, 1990 for details of traits associated with leadership.

4 Gardner, 1990, xii

5 Abigail Adam's letters to Thomas Jefferson, 1790. As quoted
    in Gardner, 1990, 39.

6 Greenleaf, 1970, 19

7 Hillman, 1999, 165

8 Rost, 1993

9 Gardner, 1990, xiv.

10 Heifetz, 1994, 251

11 c.f. Gardner, 1986, 1990; Kelley, 1992; Rost, 1993

12 Burns, 1978, 426

13 see Chaleff, 1995; Kelley, 1992 for an excellent discussion of active, rather than passive, followers

14 Rost, 1993

15 Barker, 1992

16 See Adler, 1997; House, 1995; Rost, 1993; Zaleznik, 1990; Bass, 1985; Bennis and Nanus, 1985; Conger and Kanungo, 1987; Kouzes and Posner, 1987; Peters and Waterman, 1982; Tichy and Devanna, 1986.

17 Hickman, 1990; Kotter, 1988; Yukl, 1994

18 c.f. Burns, 1978; Bass, 1985; Bennis and Nanus, 1985

19 For a discussion of leaders as visionaries, see Nanus, 1995. For a discussion of leaders as change agents, see Kanter 1983.

20 Burns, 1978, 20

21 Spears, 1998

22 Ibid., 1).

23 Greenleaf, 1996, 163.

24 As quoted in Drucker's foreword to *On Becoming a Servant Leader*, 1996b, xii.

25 See Kouzes and Posner 1993; Rost, 1993.

26 Rost, 1993, 123

27 Burns, 1978, 20

28 Ibid, 20

29 Ibid, 462

30 Bass and Avolio, 1988

31 Burns, 1978, 425

32 Kouzes and Posner, 1993, 3.

33 Gardner, 1990, 36.

CHAPTER 1: THE SEARCH FOR "LEADERSHIP"

34 Kirkpatrick and Locke, 1991

35 Leadership traits of Kouzes and Posner, 1993.

36 Hackman and Johnson, 1996

37 Hosking and Morley, 1998, 91

38 Rost, 1993, 102

39 Rost, 1993b.

40 Kouzes and Posner, 1993, 11

41 Rost, 1993, 115

42 Ibid., 118

CHAPTER 2: ENVISION

43 Deetz, Tracy, and Simpson, 2000, 56.

44 Nanus, 1996.

45 Conger and Kanungo, 1998, 154.

46 Ibid., 156.

47 House, 1995, 156.

48 Nutt and Backoff, 1997, 312.

49 Nanus, 1995, 8.

50 Yukl, 1998, 443. Yukl reviewed Bennis and Nanus, 1985; Kotter, 1996; Kouzes and Posner, 1995; Nanus, 1992;Tichy and Devanna, 1986.

51 Farace, Monge, and Russell, 1977, 16.

52 Thomas, 1976, pp.246-247

53 Nanus, 1992; Yukl, 1998.

54 Katzenbach, 1995, 71.

55 Yukl, 1998, 443.

56 Katzenbach, 1995, 68.

57 Ibid.

58 Conger and Kanungo, 1998, title of chapter 4, 121.

59 Senge, 1990b.

60 Conger and Kanungo, 1998, 138.

61 Ibid., 142.

62 Bennis and Nanus, 1985, 96.

63 Kouzes and Posner, 1987, 115

64 Bennis and Nanus, 1985, 109

65 Bennis and Goldsmith, 1997, 3

66 Nanus, 1992, xviii

67 Yukle, 1998, 445.

68 Senge, 1990, 48.

69 Yukl, 1994, pp. 103-104.

70 Yukl, 1998, 445.

71 Conger and Kanungo, 1998, 132.

72 Ibid., title of chapter 4, 121.

73 Tichy and Devanna, 1986

74 Katzenbach, 1995, 91.

75 Nanus, 1992, 21, 29

76 Snyder and Graves, 1994.

CHAPTER 3: ENLIST

77 Congo and Kanungo, 1998, 18.

78 Ibid.

79 Gardner, 1990, 28-29.

80 I highly recommend this book on interviewing: C. J. Stewart, and W.B. Cash Jr. *Interviewing: Principles and Practices,* 8th ed. Boston: MCGraw Hill, 1997.

81 Check out these texts if you are interested in facilitation, running better meetings, or creative processes in small groups: Edward DeBono. *Serious Creativity.* New York: Harper Collins, 1992.
Michael Doyle and David Straus. *How to Make Meetings Work.* New York: Berley Books, 1993.
Roger Fisher and William Ury. *Getting To Yes.* New York: Penguin, 1981.
John Gastil. *Democracy in Small Groups.* Philidelphia: New Society Publishers, 1993.

Barbara Gray. *Collaborating.* San Francisco: Jossey-Bass, 1989.

V. H. Howard and J. H Barton. *Thinking Together.* New York: William Morrow, 1992.

Johnna L. Howell. *Tools for Facilitating Team Meetings.* Seattle: Integrity Publishing, 1995.

Marjorie Parker. *Creating Shared Vision.* Claredon Hills, IL: Dialogue International, Ltd., 1990.

Lynn Kearny. *The Facilitator's Tool Kit.* Amherst, MA: HRD Press, 1995.

Michael Schrage. *Shared Minds: The New Technologies of Collaboration.* New York: Random House, 1990.

82 S. Kaner. *Facilitator's Guide to Participatory Decision-Making.* Gabriola Island, BC: New Society Publishers, 1996.

83 C.f. Shamir et al., 1993

84 C.f. Avolio and Bass, 1988; Bass 1985; Nanus, 1992

85 Congo and Kanungo, 1998, 177.

86 See Cheney, 1999; Meglino, Ravlin, and Adkins, 1989; O'Reilly, Chatman, and Caldwell, 1991; McDonald and Gandz, 1992.

87 Shamir et al., 1993

88 Safire, 1997, 538-544.

89 Congo & Kanungo, 1998, 53.

90 Gardner, 1995, 14.

91 Ibid., 43.

CHAPTER 4: EMBODY

92 This is the main assertion to Kouzes and Posner's book *Credibility*.

93 Ibid.

94 Gardner, 1995

95 Bass, 1990.

96 Bennett, 1964, 127.

97 Kouzes, 1998, 323.

98 Gardner, 1995.

99 I have developed these questions from a life-time of reading Personal-improvement texts.

100 C.f. Kirkpatrick and Lowe, 1991.

101 Kouzes and Posner, 1993

102 Kouzes and Posner, 1993; Kelley, 1992

103 C.f. Stogdill, 1948; Kirkpatrick and Locke, 1991

104 Kelley, 1992.

105 Congo and Kanungo, 1998, 189-193.

106 Gardner, 1995, 293.

107 Conger and Kanungo, 1998, 61

108 Nanus, 1992, 139.

109 Gardner, 1990.

110 Kouzes and Posner, 1993, 9.

CHAPTER 5: EMPOWER

111 C.f. Westenholz, 1993.

112 See Kelley, 1992.

113 Chile and Zorn, 1995.

114 Howard, 1998, 202

115 Freeman and Rogers, 1999, 4.

116 Theriault, 1995, 175.

117 Cheney, 1999, 160.

118 Arnold and Plas, 22.

119 Cappelli and Rogovski, 1993.

120 Bradford and Cohen, 1985; Kouzes and Posner, 1990;
     Peters and Austin, 1985; Peters and Waterman, 1982.

121 House, 1995; Howard and Wellins, 1994; Lawler, 1992;
     Thomas and Velthouse, 1990.

122 Bennis, 1984, 1989; Block, 1987; Burke, 1985.

123 These first two conditions are consistent with Chile and
     Zorn's (1995) concept of "the dual nature of empowerment
     as perceived competence and perceived control," 3.

124 Albrecht, 1988.

125 Bennis, 1984, 1989; Block, 1987; Burke, 1985.

126 Burns, 1978, 425.

127 Fairholm, 1998, 63.

128 Senge, 1990.

129 Gist, 1987.

130 See Block, 1993 for organizational advice on distributing
     quality information.

131 Gilley, Boughton, and Maycunich, 1999

132 Deetz, 1995, 7.

133 These statements are from Chile and Zorn's (1995) Empowerment Instrument used for college students.

134 Karasek and Thorell, 1990.

135 Pacanowsky, 1988.

136 See Cheney, et al., 1998 for a good discussion.

137 Rock, 1991, 44 as quoted in Cheney et al., 1998, 46.

138 Mansbridge, 1973.

139 Cheney, et al., 1998, 65.

140 Ibid., 66.

141 C.f. Michels, 1962; Weber, 1978; Mansbridge, 1983.

142 Hersey and Blanchard, 1962, 1972, 1982. For relevant discussions on how much participation leaders should give in decision making, see the contingency theories of Fiedler, 1964, 1967, 1993; normative decision theory of Vroom and Yetton, 1973; decision tree ideas of Margerison and Glube, 1979; path-goal theories of House and Mitchell, 1974; life-cycle theoris of Hersey and Blanchard, 1972, 1982; and leader-member exchange theories of Graen and Scandura, 1987.

143 Barker, 1999. I highly recommend reading this text if you are interested in the social consequences of working in participative, team-based organizations.

144 Barker, 1999.

145 Ibid.

146 Deetz, 1995, 3.

147 Senge, 1990b.

148 Hammer and Champy, 1993.

149 These statements are from Chile and Zorn's (1995) Empowerment Instrument used for college students.

150 Chile and Zorn, 1995.

151 Ibid., 21.

152 Gudykunst, Ting-Toomey, and Chua, 1988.

153 Autry, 1991, 74.

154 Gardner, 1990, 116-18

155 Bandura, 1999.

156 Kouzes and Posner, 1993.

157 Levering and Milton, 1993.

158 Snyder and Graves, 1994;

159 Andriessen and Drenth, 1984, 489

160 Drucker Foundation. *The Organization of the Future*. San Francisco: Jossey-Bass, 1997, 141.

161 McGee-Cooper, 1998, 78.

162 Hackman and Johnson, 1996

163 See Bass, 1990, 341 for review of such results.

164 Pacanowsky, 1988, 374.

165 Albrecht and Bach, 1993.

166 Klaus and Bass, 1982.

167 Bach, *Communication in Complex Organizations*, 242.

168 Ibid., 243.

169 Jablin and Krone, 1994.

170 Arnold and Plas, 1993, 31.

171 Ibid., 32.

172 Howard and Wellins, 1994.

173 See Podsakoff and Schriesheim, 1985, for a comprehensive review.

174 Bandura, 1999, 184.

175 Oakley and Krug, 1991, 247.

176 Chile and Zorn, 1995.

177 This is based on Bandura's (1986) concept of self-efficacy and the necessity to receive "emotional arousal."

178 Bandura, 1999, 184.

CHAPTER 6: EVALUATE

179 Nanus, 1992; Congo and Kanungo, 1998.

180 Nanus, 1992, 160.

181 Gardner, 1990, 73.

182 Quoted in Kouzes and Posner, 1993, 15.

183 Studies quoted in Gini, 1998.

184 Quoted from his July 8, 1941 radio address and in Safire, 1997, p.526.

185 Freeman, 1992.

186 Kidder, 1996, 155. Kidder's *How Good People Make Tough Choices,* is the best book I've read on ethics. His credibility is unsurpassed, and his easy-to-read, real-world practicality and descriptions of the concept are powerful, understandable, and inspiring.

187 These two considerations parallel what Rost, 1993, calls "the ethics of the leadership process" and "the ethics of leadership content."

188 Gini, 1998, 363 on summarizing Bowie's ideas.

189 Rost, 1993, 156.

190 Ibid., 158.

191 Kidder, 16-17.

192 Ibid., 113.

193 Ibid.

194 Ibid.

195 Ibid.

196 Gert, 1970, ii. In Kidder, 1996, 90.

197 Kung, 1991, 57. In Kidder, 1996, 91.

198 Kidder, 1994

199 Rost, 176.

200 Howell and Avolio, 1998.

201 Ibid., 168.

202 Ibid.

203 Ibid., 169.

204 Kelley, 1992, 526

205 Bass and Avolio, 1990; Bass, 1990; Bass et al., 1987; Bass, 1985.

206 Ibid., 170.

207 Ibid. Emphasis added.

208 See Bass, 1990 for a discussion.

209 Rogers, 1961, 1965.

210 Grote, 1995, 18.

211 Bass, 1990, 369. See this source for a review on reluctance
     to give feedback and use of distortion.

212 Greanleaf, 1970, 13.

213 Gilley, Boughton, and Maycunich, 1999.

214 Ibid., 73.

215 See Bass, 1990, 374.

CHAPTER 7: ENCOURAGE

216 Kouzes and Posner, 1993, 30-31.

217 Wheatley, 1998, 343.

218 Conger and Kanungo, 1998, 21.

219 See Shamir et al., 1993.

220 Kouzes and Posner, 1993, 51.

221 See Podsakoff and Schriesheim for a comprehensive review.

222 See Bass, 1990, 322, for a review.

223 Gardner, 1990, xv.

224 From my article entitled, "Choosing an Education Abroad," in *Great Falls Tribune*, no. 274, February 11, 1993.

225 Elisabeth Kübler-Ross, quoted in J. Cook, *The Book of Positive Quotations*. Minneapolis: Fairview Press, 1993.

226 Quoted in Oakley and Krug, 1991, 215.

227 This quote is from a speech in Stockholm on December 10, 1950 as quoted in Safire, 1997, 528.

CONCLUSION

228 Rost, 1993, 144.

229 Gardner, 1965, 135.

230 Kouzes and Posner, 1993, xvii.

231 Beckhard, 1996, 129.

References

Abrahamson, Eric. (1996). "Management Fashion." *Academy of Management Review* 21, no. 1: 254–85.

Albrecht, T. L. (1988). "Communication and Personal Control in Empowering Organizations." In J. A. Anderson, ed., *Communication Yearbook,* 11, 380–90. Newbury Park, CA: Sage.

Albrecht, T. L., and Betsy Wackernagel Bach (1997). *Communication in Complex Organizations: A Relational Approach.* Fort Worth: Harcourt Brace.

Allen, K. E., J. Bordas, G. Hickman, L. R. Matusak, G. J. Sorenson, and K. J. Whitmire (1998). "Leadership in the 21st Century." In G. R. Hickman, ed., *Leading Organizations: Perspectives for a New Era,* 572–80. Thousand Oaks, CA: Sage.

Alvesson, M. (1996). "Leadership Studies: From Procedure and Abstraction to Reflexivity and Situation. *Leadership Quarterly* 7: 455–85.

Anderson, P., and M. Tushman (1991). "Managing through Cycles of Technological Change. *Research Technology Management* 34 (3): 26–31.

Andriessen, E. J. H., and P. J. D. Drenth (1984). "Leadership: Theories and Models." In P. J. D. Drenth, H. Theirry et al., eds., *Handbook of Work and Organizational Psychology*. New York: Wiley.

Argyris, C. (1964). *Integrating the Individual and the Organization*. New York: Wiley.

———(1976). "Single-Loop and Double-Loop Models in Research on Decision Making. *Administrative Science Quarterly* 21(3): 363–75.

Arnold, W. W., and J. M. Plas (1993). *The Human Touch.* New York: Wiley.

Autry, J. A. (1991). *Love and Profit.* New York: Morrow.

Bandura, A. (1999). "Social Cognitive Theory of Personality." In L. A. Pervin and O. P. John, eds., *Handbook of Personality,* 2nd ed., 154–96. New York: Guilford Press.

Barciela, S. (1998). "Dharamshala Dreaming: A Traveler's Search for the Meaning of Work. In L. Spears, ed., *Insights on Leadership,* 96–116. New York: John Wiley and Sons.

Barge, J. K. (1994). *Leadership: Communication Skills for Organizations and Groups.* New York: St. Martins Press.

Barker, J. A. (1992). *Future Edge: Discovering the New Rules of Success.* New York: Morrow.

Barker, J. R. (1999). *The Discipline of Teamwork: Participation and Concertive Control.* Thousand Oaks, CA: Sage.

Barnard, C. (1938). *The Functions of the Executive.* Cambridge, MA: Harvard University Press.

Bandura, A. (1977). "Self-Efficacy: Toward a Unifying Theory of Behavioral Change. *Psychological Review* 84: 191–215.

———(1986). "The Exploratory and Predictive Scope of Self-Efficacy Theory." *Journal of Social and Clinical Psychology* 4 (3): 359–73.

Barr, P. A., J. L. Stimpert, and A. S. Huff (1992). "Cognitive Change, Strategic Action, and Organizational Renewal." *Strategic Management Journal* 13, no. 1: 15–36.

Barry, D. (1991). "Managing the Bossless Team: Lessons in Distributed Leadership." *Organizational Dynamics* 20: 31–49.

Baruch, Y. (1998). "Leadership—Is That What We Study? *Journal of Leadership Studies* 5 (1): 100–120.

Bass, Bernard M. (1985). *Leadership and Performance beyond Expectations.* New York: Free Press.

———(1990). *Bass and Stogdill's Handbook of Leadership,* 3rd ed. New York: Free Press.

————(1990b). "From Transactional to Transformational Leadership: Learning to Share the Vision." *Organizational Dynamics* 18 (3): 19–31.

Bass, B. M., and B. J. Avolio (1990). *Manual: The Multifactor Leadership Questionnaire.* Palo Alto, CA: Consulting Psychologist Press.

————(1993). "Transformational Leadership: A Response to Critiques." In M. M. Chemers and R. Aymen, eds., *Leadership Theory and Research*, 49–80. San Diego, CA: Academic Press.

Bass, B. M., B. J. Avolio, and L. Goodheim (1987). "Biography and the Assessment of Transformational Leadership at the World-Class Level." *Journal of Management* 13 (1) : 7–19.

Bass, B. M., D. A. Waldman, B. J. Avolio, and M. Bebb (1987). "Transformational Leadership and the Falling Dominoes Effect." *Group and Organization Studies* 12: 73–87.

Beer, M., R. A. Eisenstat, and B. Spector (1990). *The Critical Path to Corporate Renewal.* Boston: Harvard Business School Press.

Beckhard, R., and W. Pritchard (1992). *Changing the Essence: The Art of Creating and Leading Fundamental Change in Organizations.* San Francisco: Jossey-Bass.

Beckhard, R. (1996). "On Future Leaders." In F. Hesselbein, M. Goldsmith, and R. Beckhard, eds., *The Leader of the*

Future: New Visions, Strategies and Practices for a New Era, 125–29. San Francisco: Jossey-Bass.

Benne, K. D., and P. Sheats (1948). "Functional Roles of Group Members." *Journal of Social Issues* 4: 41–49.

Bennett, L. (1964). *What Manner of Man.* Chicago: Johnson.

Bennis, W. (1984). "The Four Competencies of Leadership. *Training and Development Journal* 38, no. 8: 14–19.

———(1989). "Why Leaders Can't Lead. *Training and Development Journal* 43, no. 4: 35–39.

Bennis, W., and B. Nannus (1985). *Leaders: The Strategies for Taking Charge.* New York: Harper and Row.

Bennis, W., and J. Goldsmith (1997). *Learning to Lead.* Reading, MA: Addison-Wesley.

Beyer, J. M., and L. D. Browning (1999). "Transforming an Industry in Crisis: Charisma, Routinization, and Supportive Cultural Leadership." *Leadership Quarterly* 10(3): 483–520.

Blake, R. R., and J. S. Mouton (1964). *The Managerial Grid.* Houston: Gulf.

Block, P. (1993). *Stewardship: Choosing Service over Self-Interest.* San Francisco: Barrett-Koehler.

———(1998). "From Leadership to Citizenship." In L. C. Spears, ed., *Insights on Leadership: Service, Stewardship, Spirit, and Servant-Leadership,* 87–95. New York: John Wiley and Sons.

————(1987). *The Empowered Manager: Positive Political Skills at Work.* San Francisco: Jossey-Bass.

Bourgeois, L. J. (1984). "Strategic Management and Determinism." *Academy of Management Review* 9, no. 4: 586–96.

Bradford, D. L., and A. R. Cohen (1985). *Managing for Excellence: The Guide to Developing High-Performance Organizations.* New York: Wiley.

Brion, J. M. (1996). *Leadership of Organizations: The Executive's Complete Handbook.* Greenwich, CT: JAI Press.

Brown, Andrew D. (1994). "Transformational Leadership in Tackling Technical Change." *Journal of General Management* 19 (4): 1–13.

Brown, S., and K. Eisenhardt (1997). "The Art of Continuous Change: Linking Complexity Theory and Time-Paced Evolution in Relentlessly Shifting Organizations." *Administrative Science Quarterly* 42: 1–34.

Burke, W. W. (1985). "Leadership as Empowering Others." In S. Srivastva, ed., *The functioning of Executive Power,* 51–77. San Francisco: Jossey-Bass.

Burns, J. M. (1978). *Leadership.* New York: Harper and Row.

Calas, M. B., and L. Smircich (1988). "Reading Leadership as a Form of Cultural Analysis. In J. G. Hunt, B. R. Baliga, H. P. Dachler, and C. A. Schriesheim, eds., *Emerging Leadership Vistas,* 201–26. Lexington, MA: Lexington Books.

Cappelli, P., and N. Rogovsky (1993). "Work Systems and Individual Performance." Mimeo. Philadelphia: National Center on the Educational Quality of the Workforce.

Cartwright, D., and A. Zander (1968). "Leadership and Performance of Group Functions: Introduction." In *Group Dynamics,* 301–17. New York: Harper and Row.

Chaleff, I. (1995). *The Courageous Follower: Standing Up To and For our Leaders.* San Francisco: Barrettt-Koehler.

Chemers, M. M. (1984). "The Social, Organizational, and Cultural Context of Effective Leadership." In B. Kellerman, ed., *Leadership: Multidisciplinary Perspectives,* 93–108. Englewood Cliffs, NJ: Prentice-Hall.

Cheney, George (1999). *Values at Work: Employee Participation Meets Market Pressures at Mondragón.* Ithaca, NY: Cornell University Press.

Cheney, G., J. Straub, L. Speirs-Glebe, C. Stohl, D. DeGooyer, S. Whalen, K. Garvin-Doxas, and D. Carlone (1998). "Democracy, Participation, and Communication at Work: A Multidisciplinary Review." In Michael E. Roloff, ed., *Communication Yearbook 21.* Thousand Oaks, CA: Sage.

Chiles, A. M., and T. Zorn (1995). "Empowerment in Organizations: Employees' Perceptions of the Influences on Empowerment." *Journal of Applied Communication Research* 23 (1): 1–25.

Coch, L., and J. R. P. French (1948). "Overcoming Resistance to Change." *Human Relations* 1 (4): 512–32.

Conger, J. A. (1989). *The Charismatic Leader: Behind the Mystique of Exceptional Leadership.* San Francisco: Jossey-Bass.

Conger, J. A., and R. N. Kanungo (1987). "Toward a Behavioral Theory of Charismatic Leadership in Organizational Settings." *Academy of Management Review* 12, no. 5: 637–47.

———(1998). *Charismatic Leadership in Organizations.* Thousand Oaks, CA: Sage.

Conger, J. A., G. M. Spreitzer, and E. E. Lawler III, eds. (1999). *The Leader's Change Handbook.* San Francisco: Jossey-Bass.

Cotton, J. L, D. A. Vollrath, K. L. Froggatt, M. L. Lengneck-Hall, and K. R. Jennings (1988). "Employee Participation: Diverse Forms and Different Outcomes." *Academy of Management Review* 13 (1): 8–22.

Covey, S. (1998). "Servant-Leadership from the Inside Out." In L. C. Spears, ed., *Insights on Leadership: Service, Stewardship, Spirit, and Servant-Leadership,* xii. New York: John Wiley and Sons.

———(1990). *Principle-Centered Leadership.* New York: Simon and Schuster (Fireside).

Cummings, T. G. (1999). "The Role and Limits of Change

Leadership. In J. A. Conger, G. M. Spreitzer, and E. E. Lawler III, eds., *The Leader's Change Handbook,* 301–20. San Francisco: Jossey-Bass.

Deetz, S. A., S. J. Tracy, and J. L. Simpson (2000). *Leading Organizations through Transition: Communication and Cultural Change,* ch. 4. Thousand Oaks, CA: Sage.

DeMeuse, K. P. (1986). "A Combination of Frequently Used Measures in Industry/Organizational Psychology." *The Industrial-Organizational Psychologist* 23, no. 2: 53–59.

DePree, M. (1993). *Leadership Jazz.* New York: Doubleday/Dell.

Drucker, P. (1992). "The New Society of Organizations." *Harvard Business Review* 70, Sept–Oct.: 95–105.

DuBrin, Andrew J. (1998). *Leadership: Research Findings, Practice, and Skills.* Boston: Houghton Mifflin.

Eblen, A. L. (1987). "Communication, Leadership, and Organizational Commitment." *Central States Speech Journal* 38 (3): 181–95.

Eddy, J. P., S. D. Murphy, D. J. Spaulding, K. V. Chandras (1997). "21st-Century Leadership Practices Needed for Higher Education. *Education* 117, Spring: 327–32.

Eden, D. (1990). *Pygmalion in Management: Productivity as a Self-Fulfilling Prophecy.* Lexington, MA: Lexington books.

Eisenburg, E. M., and H. L. Goodall Jr. (1993). *Organizational Communication: Balancing Creativity and Constraint.* New York: St. Martin's Press.

Fairholm, G. W. (1998). *Perspectives on Leadership: From the Science of Management to Its Spiritual Heart.* Westport, CT: Quorum Books.

Fairhurst, G. T., L. E. Rogers, and R. A. Sarr (1987). "Manager-Subordinate Control Patterns and Judgements about the Relationship." In M. McLaughlin, ed., *Communication Yearbook,* vol. 10, 83–116. Beverly Hills, CA: Sage.

Fairhurst, G. T., and T. A. Chandler (1989). Social Structure in Leader-Member Interaction. *Communication Monographs* 56: 213–39.

Fairhurst, G. T., and R. A. S. Sarr (1996). *The Art of Framing: Managing the Language of Leadership.* San Francisco: Jossey Bass.

Farace, R. V., P. R. Monge, and H. M. Russell (1977). *Communicating and Organizing.* New York: Random House.

Fiedler, F. (1964). "A Contingency Model of Leadership Effectiveness. In L. Berkowitz, ed., *Advances in Experimental Social Psychology,* vol 1. New York: Academic Press.

———(1967). *A Theory of Leadership Effectiveness.* New York: McGraw-Hill.

———(1993). "The Leadership Situation and the Black Box in Contingency Theories." In M. M Chemers and R. Aymen, eds., *Leadership Theory and Research: Perspectives and Directions,* 1–28. San Diego, CA: Academic Press.

Finch, F. E. (1977). "Collaborative Leadership in Work Settings. *Journal of Applied Behavioral Science* 13: 292–302.

Finley, N. E. (1998). "Spinning the Leadership Relationship Web into the Twenty-first Century." *Journal of Leadership Studies,* Winter: 51.

Fisher, B. M., and J. E. Edwards (1988). "Consideration and Initiating Structure and Their Relationships with Leader Effectiveness: A Meta-analysis." *Proceedings of the Academy of Management,* August: 201–5.

Fisher, K. (1993). *Leading Self-Directed Work Teams: A Guide to Developing New Team Leadership Skills.* New York: McGraw-Hill.

Foster, R. (2000). "Leadership in the Twenty-First Century: Working to build a Civil Society." *National Civic Review* 89, Spring: 87.

Freeman, R. E. (1992). "The Problem of the Two Realms." Speech, Loyola University, Chicago, Center for Ethics. As quoted in Gini (1998), 364.

Freeman, R. B., and J. Rogers (1999). *What Workers Want.* New York: Cornell University Press.

Gardner, J. W. (1986). *The Nature of Leadership.* Washington, DC: Independent Sector.

———(1990). *On Leadership.* New York: Free Press.

———(1965). "The Antileadership Vaccine." In *No Easy Victories,* Annual Report of the Carnegie Corporation, New York, 1965. Quoted in Bennis, W., and J. Goldsmith (1997). *Learning to Lead,* 135. Reading, MA: Addison-Wesley.

Gardner, H. (1995). *Leading Minds.* New York: Basic Books.

Gert, B. (1970). *The Moral Rules: A New Foundation for Morality.* New York: Harper and Row.

Gilley, J. W., N. W. Boughton, and A. Maycunich (1999). *The Performance Challenge.* Reading, MA: Perseus Books.

Gini, A. (1998). "Moral Leadership and Business Ethics." In G. R. Hickman, ed., *Leading Organizations: Perspectives for a New Era,* 360–71. Thousand Oaks, CA: Sage.

Ginsberg, A. (1988). "Measuring and Modeling Changes in Strategy: Theoretical Foundations and Empirical Directions." *Strategic Management Journal* 9, no. 6: 559–75.

Gist, M. E. (1987). "Self-Efficacy: Implications for Organizational Behavior and Human Resource Management." *Academy of Management Review* 12[issue no. here]: 472–85.

Greenleaf, R. K. (1970). "The Servant as Leader. In Spears, *Insights on Leadership,* 15–20.

———(1996a). *Servant and Seeker.* San Francisco: Jossey-Bass.

———(1996b). *On Becoming a Servant Leader.* San Francisco: Jossey-Bass.

Gregersen, H., A. Morrison, and J. Black (1998). "Developing Leaders for the Global Frontier." *Sloan Management Review* 40, no. 1: 21–32.

Graeff, C. L. (1997). "Evolution of Situational Leadership Theory: A Critical Review." *Leadership Quarterly* 8 (2): 153–70.

Graen, G. B., and T. A. Scandura (1987). "Toward a Psychology of Dyadic Organizing." In L. L. Cummings and B. M. Staw, eds., *Research in Organizational Behavior* 9, 175–208. New York: JAI Press.

Greanleaf, R. K. (1977). *Servant Leadership*. New York: Paulist Press.

Grint, K., ed. (1997). *Leadership: Classical, Contemporary, and Critical Approaches*. Oxford: Oxford University Press.

Greiner, L., and Schein, V. (1988). *Power and Organizational Development*. Reading, MA: Addison-Wesley.

Grote, D. (1995). *Discipline without Punishment: The Proven Strategy That Turns Problem Employees into Superior Performers*. New York: Amacom.

Gudykunst, W. B., S. Ting-Toomey, and E. Chua (1988). *Culture and Interpersonal Communication*. Newbury Park, CA: Sage.

Hackman, M. Z., and C. E. Johnson (1996). *Leadership: A Communication Perspective*. Prospect Heights, IL: Waveland Press.

Hammer, M., and J. Champy (1993). *Reengineering the Corporation*. HarperCollins.

Harper, S. C. (1998). "Leading Organization Change in the 21st Century." *Industrial Management* 40, May-June: 25–31.

Hater, J. J., and B. M. Bass (1988). "Superiors' Evaluation and Subordinates' Perceptions of Transformational and Transactional Leadership." *Journal of Applied Psychology* 73: 695–702.

Hartog, D. N. D., and R. M. Vergurg (1997). "Charisma and Rhetoric: Communicative Techniques of International Business Leaders." *Leadership Quarterly* 8 (4): 355–91.

Heifetz, R. A. (1994). *Leadership without Easy Answers.* Cambridge, MA: Harvard University Press.

Hersey, P., and K. H. Blanchard (1982). *Management of Organizational Behavior,* 4th ed. Englewood Cliffs, NJ: Prentice-Hall.

Hesselbein, F., M. Goldsmith, and R. Beckhard, eds. (1997). *The Organization of the Future.* San Francisco: Jossey-Bass.

———(1996). *The Leader of the Future.* San Francisco: Jossey-Bass.

Hickman, C. R. (1990). *Mind of a Manager, Soul of a Leader.* Englewood Cliffs, NJ: Prentice-Hall.

Hickman, G. R. (1998). "Leadership and the Social Imperative of Organizations in the 21st Century." In G. R. Hickman, ed., *Leading Organizations: Perspectives for a New Era,* 559–71. Thousand Oaks, CA: Sage.

Hillman, J. (1999). *The Force of Character.* New York: Random House.

Hosking, D. M., and I. E. Morley (1988). "The Skills of Leadership." In J. G. Hunt, B. R. Baliga, H. P. Dachler, and C. A. Schriesheim, eds., *Emerging Leadership Vistas,* 89–106. Lexington, MA: Lexington Books.

House, R. J. (1971). "A Path-Goal Theory of Leader Effectiveness." *Administrative Science Quarterly* 16: 321–38.

————(1995). "Leadership in the Twenty-first Century: A Speculative Inquiry." In A. Howard, ed., *The Changing Nature of Work,* 411–50. San Francisco: Jossey-Bass.

————(1996). "Path-Goal Theory Revisited: Lessons, Legacy, and a Reformulated Theory." *Leadership Quarterly* 7: 323–52.

House, R. J., and T. R. Mitchell (1974). "Path-Goal Theory of Leadership." *Journal of Contemporary Business* 3 (4): 81–97.

Howard, A., and R. S. Wellins (1994). *High-Involvement Leadership: Changing Roles for Changing Times.* Pittsburgh, PA: Development Dimensions International.

Howard, A. (1998). "The Empowering Leader: Unrealized Opportunities." In G. R. Hickman. ed., *Leading Organizations,* 202–13.

Howell, J., and B. J. Avolio (1998). "The Ethics of Charismatic Leadership: Submission or Liberation." In G. R. Hickman, *Leading Organizations,* 166–76.

Hunt, J. G. (1984). "Organizational Leadership: The Contingency Paradigm and Its Challenges. In B. Kellerman, ed., *Leadership: Multidisciplinary Perspective.* Englewood Cliffs, NJ: Prentice-Hall.

Ireland, R. D., and M. A. Hitt (1999). "**Achieving and Maintaining Strategic Competitiveness in the 21st Century: The Role of Strategy Leadership.**" (Special Issue: Global Competitiveness, part 2). *The Academy of Management Executive* 13, February: 43–44.

Jablin, F. M., and K. J. Krone (1994). "Task/Work Relationships: A Life-Span Perspective." In Knapp, Mark L., and G. R. Miller, eds., *Handbook of Interpersonal Communication.* Beverly Hills, CA: Sage.

Jeffries, E. (1998). "Work as a Calling." In Spears, *Insights on Leadership.*

Kahn, R., and D. Katz (1960). "Leadership Practices in Relation to Productivity and Morale." In D. Cartwright and A. Zander, eds., *Group Dynamics: Research and Theory.* Elmsford, NY: Row, Peterson.

Kanter, R. M. (1983). *The Change Masters.* Simon and Schuster.

Karasek, R., and T. Theorell (1990). *Healthy Work: Stress, Productivity, and the Reconstruction of Working Life.* New York: Basic Books.

Kellerman, B. (1984). "Leadership as a Political Act." In B. Kellerman, ed., *Leadership: Multidisciplinary Perspectives,* 63–89. Englewood Cliffs, NJ: Prentice-Hall.

Kelley, R. E. (1992). *The Power of Followership.* New York: Doubleday.

Kidder, R. M. (1996). *How Good People Make Tough Choices.* New York: Fireside.

———(1994). *Shared Values for a Troubled World: Conversations with Men and Women of Conscience.* San Francisco: Jossey-Bass.

Klauss, R., and B. M. Bass (1982). *Interpersonal Communication in Organizations*. New York: Academic Press.

Krech, D., and R. Crutchfield (1948). *Theory and Problems in Social Psychology*. New York: McGraw-Hill.

Kirkpatrick, S. A., and E. A. Locke (1991). "Leadership: Do Traits Matter?" *Academy of Management Executive* 5 (2): 48–60.

Kotter, J. P. (1995). "Leading Change: Why Transformational Efforts Fail." *Harvard Business Review*, March–April: 59–67.

———(1990a). "What Leaders Really Do." *Harvard Business Review*, May–June.

———(1990b). *A Force for Change: How Leadership Differs from Management*. New York: Free Press.

———(1988). *The Leadership Factor*. New York: Free Press.

Kouzes, J. M., and B. Z. Posner (1987). *The Leadership Challenge*. San Francisco: Jossey-Bass.

———(1993). *Credibility*. San Francisco: Jossey-Bass.

Kouzes, J. (1998). "Finding Your Voice. In Spears, *Insights on Leadership*.

Kung, H. (1991). *Global Responsibility: In Search of a New World Ethic*. New York: Crossroad Publishing Company.

Kuratko, D. F., and J. S. Hornsby (1998). "Corporate Entrepreneurial Leadership for the 21st Century." *Journal of Leadership Studies* 5, Spring: 27.

Lawler, E. E. I. (1992). *The Ultimate Advantage: Creating the High-Involvement Organization*. San Francisco: Jossey-Bass.

Leavitt, H. J. (1986). *Corporate Pathfinders.* New York: Dow-Jones-Irwin and Penguin Books.

Levering, R., and M. Moskowitz (1993). *The 100 Best Companies to Work for in America.* New York: Currency/Doubleday.

Lewin, K. (1951). *Field Theory in Social Science: Selected Theoretical Papers.* D. Cartwright, ed. New York: Harper and Row.

Lewis, C. P. (1997). *Building a Shared Vision: A Leader's Guide to Aligning the Organization.* Portland, OR: Productivity Press.

Lipman-Blumen, J. (1992). "Connective Leadership: Female Leadership Styles in the 21st Century Workplace." *Sociological Perspectives* 35 (1): 183–203.

Mansbridge, J. (1973). "Time, Emotion, and Inequality: Three Problems of Participatory Groups." *Journal of Applied Behavioral Science* 9 (2/3): 351–68.

———(1983). *Beyond Adversary Democracy.* Chicago: University of Chicago Press.

Manz, C. C., and H. P. Sims Jr. (1980). "Self–Management as a Substitute for Leadership: A Social Learning Perspective." *Academy of Management Review* 5 (3): 361–67.

———(1987). "Leading Workers to Lead Themselves: The External Leadership of Self-Managing Work Teams." *Administrative Science Quarterly* 32 (1): 106–28.

———(1989). *SuperLeadership: Leading Others to Lead Themselves.* New York: Prentice-Hall.

————(1993). *Business without Bosses*. New York: Wiley.

Manz, C. C., D. E. Keeting, and A. Donnellon (1990). "Preparing for an Organizational Change to Employee Self-Management: The Managerial Transition." *Organizational Dynamics,* Autumn: 15–26.

Margerison, C., and R. Glube (1979). "Leadership Decision Making: An Empirical Test of the Vroom and Yetton Model." *Journal of Management Studies* 16: 45–55.

McDonald, P., and J. Gandz (1992). "Getting Value from Shared Values. *Organizational Dynamics*, 20 (3), 64–76.

McGee-Cooper, A. (1998). "Accountability as Covenant: The Taproot of Servant-Leadership." In Spears, *Insights on Leadership*.

Meglino, B., C. Ravlin, and C. L. Adkins (1989). "A Work Values Approach to Corporate Culture." *Journal of Applied Psychology* 74 (3): 424–32.

Meindle, J. R. (1990). "On Leadership: An Alternative to the Conventional Wisdom." In B. A. Staw, ed., *Research in Organizational Behavior,* vol. 12, 160–203. New York: JAI Press.

Meindle, J. R., and S. B. Ehrlich (1987). "The Romance of Leadership and the Evaluation of Organizational Performance." *Academy of Management Journal* 30 (1): 91–109.

Melendez, S.E. (1996). "An 'Outsider's' View of Leadership." In Hesselbein, F., M. Goldsmith, and R. Beckhard, eds., *The Leader of the Future,* 293–302. San Francisco: Jossey-Bass.

Meyerson, M. (1997). *Everything I Thought I Knew About Leadership Is Wrong.* Fast Company, Special Edition.

Miller, D., and P. H. Friesen (1978). Archetypes of Strategy Formulation. *Management Science* 24, no. 9: 921–33.

———(1980a). "Momentum and Revolution in Organizational Adaptation." *Academy of Management Journal* 23, no. 4: 591–614.

———(1980b). "Archetypes or Organizational Transition." *Administrative Science Quarterly* 25, no. 2: 268–99.

———(1982). The Longitudinal Analysis of Organizations: A Methodological Perspective." *Management Science* 28, no. 9: 1013–34.

———(1984). *Organizations: A Quantum View.* Englewood Cliffs, NJ: Prentice-Hall.

Miller, K. I., and P. R. Monge (1986). "Participation, Satisfaction, and Productivity: A Meta-analytic Review." *Academy of Management Journal* 29 (4): 727–53.

Mintzberg, H., and F. Westley (1992). "Cycles of Organizational Change." *Strategic Management Journal* 13, no. 1: 39–59.

Michels, R. (1962). *Political Parties: A Sociological Study of the Oligarchical Tendencies of Modern Bureaucracy,* E. Paul and Paul, trans. New York: Collier.

Morgan, G. (1986). *Images of Organization.* Beverly Hills, CA: Sage.

Morrison, E. K. (1994). *Leadership Skills: Developing Volunteers for Organizational Success.* Tucson, AZ: Fisher Books.

Nadler, D., and M. Nadler (1997). *Champions of Change.* San Francisco: Jossey-Bass.

Nadler, D. A., and M. L. Tushman (1990). "Beyond the Charismatic Leader: Leadership and Organizational Change." *California Management Review,* Winter: 77–97.

———(1989). "Organizational Frame Bending: Principles for Managing Reorientation." *Academy of Management Review* 3, no. 3: 194–205.

Nanus, B. (1995). *Visionary Leadership.* San Francisco: Jossey-Bass.

———(1996). *Leading the Way to Organizational Renewal.* Portland, OR: Productivity Press.

Northouse, P. G. (1997). *Leadership: Theory and Practice.* Thousand Oaks, CA, Sage.

Novelli, L. Jr., and S. Taylor (1993). "The Context for Leadership in 21st-Century Organizations: A Role for Critical Thinking." *American Behavioral Scientist* 37, September–October: 139–48.

Nutt, P. C., and R. W. Backoff (1997). "Crafting Vision." *Journal of Management Inquiry* 6, no. 4: 308–28.

Oakley, E., and D. Krug (1991). *Enlightened Leadership: Getting to the Heart of Change.* New York: Fireside.

O'Connor, R. M. (1997). "The Role of Communication in Leadership Process." In P. Y. Byers, ed., *Organizational*

Communication: Theory and Behavior, 117–45. Boston: Allyn and Bacon.

O'Reilly, C. A., J. Chatman, and D. Caldwell (1991). "People and Organizational Culture: A Profile Comparison Approach to Assessing Person-Organization Fit." *Academy of Management Journal* 34 (3): 487–516.

Pacanowsky, M. (1988). "Communication in the Empowering Organization." In J. A. Anderson, ed., *Communication Yearbook* 11, 356–79. Newbury Park, CA: Sage.

Pacetta, F. (1994). *Don't Fire them, Fire Them Up.* New York: Simon and Schuster.

Peters, T., and N. Austin (1985). *A Passion for Excellence: The Leadership Difference.* New York: Warner.

Peters, T. J., and R. H. Waterman Jr. (1982). *In Search of Excellence.* New York: Harper and Row.

Podsakoff, P.M., and Schriesheim, C.A. (1985). "Leader Reward and Punishment Behavior: A Methodological and Substantive Review." In B. Staw and L. L. Cummings, eds., *Research in Organizational Behavior.* San Francisco: Jossey-Bass.

Popper, M., and E. Zakkai (1994). "Transactional, Charismatic, and Transformational Leadership: Conditions Conducive to their Predominance." *Leadership and Organization Development Journal* 15(6): 3–7.

Reeves, T., J. W. Duncan, and P. M. Ginter (2000). "Leading Change by Managing Paradoxes." *Journal of Leadership Studies* 7, Winter: 13.

Remland, M. S. (1984). "Leadership Impressions and Non-verbal Communication in a Superior-Subordinate Interaction." *Communication Quarterly* 32: 41–48.

Roby, P. A. (1998). "Creating a Just World: Leadership for the Twenty-first Century." *Social Problems* 45 (1): February: 1–20.

Rock, C. R. (1991). "Workplace Democracy in the United States." In J. D. Wisman, ed., *Worker Empowerment: The Struggle for Workplace Democracy,* 37–58. New York: Bootstrap.

Rogers, C. R. (1961). *On Becoming a Person.* Boston: Houghton Mifflin.

———(1965). *Client-Centered Therapy: Its Current Practice, Implication, and Theory.* Boston: Houghton Mifflin.

Rost, J. C. (1993). *Leadership in the Twenty-First Century.* Westport, CT: Praeger Press.

———(1993b). "Leadership Development in the New Millennium." *Journal of Leadership Studies* 1, no. 1: 109–110.

Safire, W. (1997). *Lend Me Your Ears: Great Speeches in History.* New York: W. W. Norton.

Schor, Juliet B. (1992). *The Overworked American.* New York: Basic Books.

Schriesheim, C. A., and S. Kerr (1977). "Theories and Measures of Leadership: A Critical Appraisal." In J. G. Hunt and L. L. Larson, eds., *Leadership: The Cutting Edge,* 9–45. Carbondale, IL: Southern Illinois University Press.

Schultz, B. (1986). "Communication Correlates of Perceived Leaders in the Small Group." *Small Group Behavior* 17: 51–65.

Senge, P. M. (1990). "The Leader's New Work: Building a Learning Organization." *Sloan Management Review,* Fall: 7–23.

————(1990b). *The Fifth Discipline: The Art and Practice of a Learning Organization.* New York: Doubleday.

Sennett, Richard (1998). *The Corrosion of Character: The Personal Consequences of Work in the New Capitalism.* New York: WW Norton.

Serafini, D. M., and J. C. Pearson (1984). "Leadership Behavior and Sex Role Socialization: Two Sides of the Same Coin." *Southern Communication Journal* 49: 396–405.

Sergiovanni, T. J. (1990). *Value-Added Leadership.* San Diego: Harcourt Brace.

Shamir, B., R. House, and M. B. Arthur (1993). "The Motivational Effects of Charismatic Leadership: A Self-Concept Based Theory." *Organization Science* 4, no. 4: 577–94.

Singer, M. S., and A. E. Singer (1990). "Situational Contraints on Transformational Versus Transactional Leadership Behavior, Subordinate's Leadership Preference, and Satisfaction." *Journal of Social Psychology* 130: 385–96.

Smith, K. K. (1982). "Philosophical Problems in Thinking about Organizational Change." In P. S. Goodman and Associates, eds., *Change in Organizations: New Perspectives on Theory, Research, and Practice.* San Francisco: Jossey-Bass.

Smith, P. B., and M. F. Peterson (1988). *Leadership, Organizations, and Culture.* Beverly Hills, CA: Sage.

Snyder, N. H., and M. Graves (1994). "Leadership and Vision." *Business Horizons* 37, January–February: 1–7.

Spears, L. C., ed. (1998). *Insights on Leadership: Service, Stewardship, Spirit, and Servant-Leadership.* New York: John Wiley and Sons.

Stodgill, R. M. (1948). "Personal Factors Associated with Leadership: A Survey of the Literature." *Journal of Psychology* 25: 35–71.

————(1974). *Handbook of Leadership.* New York: Free Press.

Strube, M. J., and J. E. Garcia (1981). "A Meta-Analytical Investigation of Fiedler's Contingency Model of Leadership Effectiveness." *Psychological Bulletin* 90 (2): 307–21.

Theriault, Reg (1995). *How to Tell When You're Tired: A Brief Examination of Work.* New York: W. W. Norton.

Thomas, B. (1976). *Walt Disney: An American Tradition.* New York: Simon and Shuster.

Thomas, K. W., and B. A. Velthouse (1990). "Cognitive Elements of Empowerment: An 'Interpretive' Model of Intrinsic Task Motivation." *Academy of Management review* 15, no. 4: 666–81.

Tichy, N. M., and M. A. De Vanna (1990). *The Transformational Leader.* New York: John Wiley and Sons.

Tichy, N. M., and D. O. Ulrich (1984). "SMR Forum: The Leadership Challenge—A Call for the Transformational Leader." *Sloan Management Review,* Fall: 59–68.

Todd, M. J. (1996). "21st Century Leadership and Technology." *Journal of Management in Engineering* 12, July–August: 40–50.

Tucker, J. H. (1983). "Leadership Orientation as a Function of Interpersonal Need Structure: A Replication with Negative Results." *Small Group Behavior* 14 (1): 107–14.

Tushman, M. L., W. H. Newman, and E. Romanelli (1986). "Convergence and Upheaval: Managing the Unsteady Pace of Organizational Evolution." *California Management Review* 29, no. 1: 29–44.

Vecchio, R. P. (1982). "A Further Test of Leadership Effects Due to Between-Group Variation and within-in Group Variation." *Journal of Applied Psychology* 67: 200–208.

Vecchio, R. (1987). "Situational Leadership Theory: An Examiniation of a Prescriptive Theory." *Journal of Applied Psychology* 72: 444–51.

Vroom, V. H., and A. G. Jago (1988). *The New Leadership: Managing Participation in Organizations.* Englewood Cliffs, NJ: Prentice-Hall.

Vroom, V. H., and P. W. Yetton (1973). *Leadership and Decision Making.* Pittsburgh, PA: Pittsburgh Press.

Wagner, J. A. III., and R. Z. Gooding (1987). "Shared Influence and Organizational Behavior: A Meta-analysis of
Situational Variables Expected to Moderate Participation-
Outcome Relationships." *Academy of Management Journal*
30 (3): 524–41.

Waldman, D. A., T. Lituchy, M. Gopalakrishnan, K. Lafram-
boise, B. Galperin, and Z. Kaltsounakis (1998). "A Quali-
tatitive Analysis of Leadership and Quality Improvement."
Leadership Quarterly 9: 177–201.

Wheatley, M. (1998). "What Is Our Work." In Spears, *Insights
on Leadership*, 340–51.

Weber, M. (1978). *Economy and Society: An Outline of Interpretive Sociology*, vols. 1, 2, G. Roth and C. Wittich, trans.
Berkeley, CA: University of California Press.

Westenholz, A. (1993). "Paradoxical Thinking and Change in the
Frames of Reference." *Organization Studies* 14 (1): 37–58.

Wieck, K. E. (1978). "The Spines of Leaders." In M. McCall
and M. Lombardo, eds., *Leadership: Where Else Can We Go?*
37–61. Durham, NC: Duke University Press.

Willingham, R. (1987). *Integrity Selling*. New York: Doubleday.

Wren, J. T., ed. (1995). *The Leaders Companion: Insights on
Leadership through the Ages*. New York: Free Press.

Yammarino, F. J., and B. M. Bass (1990). "Transformational
Leadership with Multiple Levels of Analysis. *Human Relations* 43 (10): 975–95.

Yukl, G. (1994). *Leadership in Organizations,* 3rd ed. Englewood Cliffs, NJ: Prentice-Hall.

———(1981). *Leadership in Organizations.* Englewood Cliffs,
NJ: Prentice-Hall.

Zorn, T. E. (1991). "Construct System Development, Transformational Leadership and Leadership Messages." *Southern
Communication Journal* 56: 178–93.

Zorn, T. E., L. T. Christensen, and G. Cheney (1999). *Constant
Change and Flexibility: Do We Really Want This?* Beyond the
Bottom Line series, vol. 2. San Francisco: Barrett-Koehler.

Zorn, T. E., and G. B. Leichty (1991). "Leadership and Identity: A Reinterpretation of Situational Leadership Theory.
Southern Communication Journal 56: 11–24.

Zorn, T. E., D. J. Page, and G. Cheney (2000). "Multiple
Perspectives on Change-Oriented Communication in a
Public-Sector Organization." *Management Communication
Quarterly* 13 (4): 515–66.

READER NOTES

_____

_____

_____

_____

_____

_____

_____

_____

_____

_____

_____

_____

_____

_____

CPSIA information can be obtained
at www.ICGtesting.com
Printed in the USA
BVOW09s0925250418
514390BV00001B/52/P